M

DECONSTRUCTIVIST ARCHITECTURE

DECONSTRUCTIVIST ARCHITECTURE

The exhibition and catalogue are part of the

Gerald D. Hines Interests Architecture Program

at The Museum of Modern Art, New York

DECON- STRUC- TIVIST ARCHI- TECTURE

Philip Johnson and Mark Wigley

The Museum of Modern Art, New York

Distributed by New York Graphic Society Books

Little, Brown and Company, Boston

Published on the occasion of the exhibition
"Deconstructivist Architecture," June 23–August 30, 1988,
directed by Philip Johnson, guest curator, and Mark Wigley,
associate curator, assisted by Frederieke Taylor

Library of Congress Catalogue Card Number 88-60826
ISBN 0-87070-298-X

Edited by James Leggio
Designed by James Wageman
Production by Susan Schoenfeld
Set in type by Concept Typographic Services, New York
Printed by Eastern Press, New Haven, Connecticut
Bound by Sendor Bindery, New York

Distributed outside the United States and Canada by
Thames and Hudson Ltd., London

The Museum of Modern Art
11 West 53 Street
New York, New York 10019

Printed in the United States of America

Cover: Detail of a project sketch by
Coop Himmelblau, transmitted by fax

Contents

Foreword

This book is published on the occasion of the exhibition "Deconstructivist Architecture," the third of five exhibitions in the Gerald D. Hines Interests Architecture Program at The Museum of Modern Art.

It is with great pleasure that we welcome back Philip Johnson as the guest curator of the exhibition. Having founded the Department of Architecture and Design in 1932, Philip Johnson was also responsible for many of the early landmark exhibitions organized by the department, including "Modern Architecture: International Exhibition" in 1932, "Machine Art" in 1934, and "Mies van der Rohe" in 1947. This is the first exhibition he has done since 1954, when he relinquished the directorship of the department, though the Museum has had the good fortune of having him serve as a Trustee since 1957. He also served as Chairman of the Trustee Committee on Architecture and Design until 1981, and since then has been Honorary Chairman of the Committee. His critical eye and keen ability to discern emerging directions in architecture have once again produced a provocative exhibition. We are also grateful to Mark Wigley, who has been Philip Johnson's associate in organizing the exhibition, and to the seven architects whose work is featured, for their enthusiastic cooperation.

Finally, we would like to extend our thanks once again to the Gerald D. Hines Interests for their generosity and vision in making this series on contemporary architecture possible.

Stuart Wrede
Director, Department of Architecture and Design

Preface

It is now about sixty years since Henry-Russell Hitchcock, Alfred Barr, and I started our quest for a new style of architecture which would, like Gothic or Romanesque in their day, take over the discipline of our art. The resulting exhibition of 1932, "Modern Architecture," summed up the architecture of the twenties—Mies van der Rohe, Le Corbusier, Gropius, and Oud were the heroes—and prophesied an International Style in architecture to take the place of the romantic "styles" of the previous half century.

With this exhibition, there are no such aims. As interesting to me as it would be to draw parallels to 1932, however delicious it would be to declare again a new style, that is not the case today. Deconstructivist architecture is not a new style. We arrogate to its development none of the messianic fervor of the modern movement, none of the exclusivity of that catholic and Calvinist cause. Deconstructivist architecture represents no movement; it is not a creed. It has no "three rules" of compliance. It is not even "seven architects."

It is a confluence of a few important architects' work of the years since 1980 that shows a similar approach with very similar forms as an outcome. It is a concatenation of similar strains from various parts of the world.

Since no forms come out of nowhere, but are inevitably related to previous forms, it is perhaps not strange that the new forms of deconstructivist architecture hark back to Russian Constructivism of the second and third decades of this century. I am fascinated by these formal similarities, of our architects to each other, on the one hand, and to the Russian movement on the other. Some of these similarities are unknown to the younger architects themselves, let alone premeditated.

Take the most obvious formal theme repeated by every one of the artists: the diagonal overlapping of rectangular or trapezoidal bars. These are also quite clear in the work of all of the Russian avant-garde from Malevich to Lissitzky. The similarity, for example, of Tatlin's warped planes and Hadid's is obvious. The "lini-ism" of Rodchenko comes out in Coop Himmelblau and Gehry, and so on.

The changes that shock the eye of an old modernist like myself are the contrasts between the "warped" images of deconstructivist architecture and the "pure" images of the old International Style. Two favorite icons of mine come to mind:

a ball bearing, featured on the cover of the catalogue of The Museum of Modern Art's "Machine Art" exhibition, in 1934, and a photograph taken recently by Michael Heizer of an 1860s spring house on his property in the Nevada desert.

Both icons were "designed" by anonymous persons for purely non-aesthetic aims. Both seem significantly beautiful in their respective eras. The first image fitted our thirties ideals of machine beauty of form, unadulterated by "artistic" designers. The photo of the spring house strikes the same chord in the brain today as the ball bearing did two generations ago. It is my receiving eye that has changed.

Think of the contrasts. The ball bearing form represents clarity, perfection; it is single, clear, platonic, severe. The image of the spring house is disquieting, dislocated, mysterious. The sphere is pure; the jagged planks make up a deformed space. The contrast is between perfection and violated perfection.

The same phenomenon as in architecture is happening in painting and sculpture. Many artists who do not copy from one another, who are obviously aware of Russian Constructivism, make shapes akin to deconstructivist architectural forms. The intersecting "cones and pillars" of Frank Stella, the trapezoidal earth lines of Michael Heizer, and the sliced, warped volumes of a Ken Price cup come to mind.

In art as well as architecture, however, there are many—and contradictory—trends in our quick-change generation. In architecture, strict-classicism, strict-modernism, and all sorts of shades in between, are equally valid. No generally persuasive "-ism" has appeared. It may be none will arise unless there is a worldwide, new religion or set of beliefs out of which an aesthetic could be formed.

Meanwhile pluralism reigns, perhaps a soil in which poetic, original artists can develop.

The seven architects represented in the exhibition, born in seven different countries and working in five different countries today, were not chosen as the sole originators or the only examples of deconstructivist architecture. Many good designs were necessarily passed over in making this selection from what is still an ever-growing phenomenon. But these seven architects seemed to us a fair cross-section of a broad group. The confluence may indeed be temporary; but its reality, its vitality, its originality can hardly be denied.

Left: Self-aligning ball bearing. 1929. Steel, 8½" (21.5 cm) diameter. The Museum of Modern Art, New York; Gift of SKF Industries

Below: Spring house, Nevada. 1860s

The person responsible for bringing this exhibition into existence is the Director of the Department of Architecture and Design, Stuart Wrede. He generously invited me to be guest curator of the exhibition and since then has been an authoritative and caring leader, sacrificing time from his own tight schedule to devote energy and direction to ours.

There could have been no exhibition or book without the contribution of my associate, Mark Wigley of Princeton University, theorist, architect, and teacher. In every field, from concept to installation, his judgment, knowledge, and hard work have been paramount.

Assisting myself and him has been Frederieke Taylor, coordinator of the exhibition. Her tireless work, tactfulness, and patient loyalty to the project were irreplaceable.

To Debbie Taylor, my gratitude for her dedication and organizational efficiency; also to John Burgee and his staff for helpful criticism and support.

At the Museum I owe thanks to my co-workers on the publication staff: most especially the editor, James Leggio; also Bill Edwards, Tim McDonough, and Susan Schoenfeld; and the designer, Jim Wageman. In addition, the following individuals contributed to the realization of the exhibition: Jerome Neuner, Production Manager, Exhibition Program; Richard L. Palmer, Coordinator of Exhibitions; James S. Snyder, Deputy Director for Planning and Program Support; Sue B. Dorn, Deputy Director for Development and Public Affairs; Lynne Addison, Associate Registrar; Jeanne Collins, Director of Public Information; and Priscilla Barker, Director of Special Events.

My thanks also to William Rubin, Director of Painting and Sculpture; John Elderfield, Director of Drawings; Riva Castleman, Director of Prints and Illustrated Books; and John Szarkowski, Director of Photography, who so generously lent paintings, drawings, prints, and photographs from the Museum's collection of Constructivist art. Magdalena Dabrowski, Assistant Curator in the Department of Drawings, was especially helpful with our research of the Constructivist work.

We also thank the following institutions, which so kindly lent works from their collections: the Museum für angewandte Kunst, Vienna; the Senator für Bau- und Wohnungswesen, I.B.A. Archive, Berlin; and Land Hessen, represented by the Staatsbauamt, Frankfurt am Main. Coop Himmelblau wishes to express their gratitude to EWE Küchen, Wels, Austria, for financial assistance in transporting their project models. Lastly, on behalf of Peter Eisenman and Daniel Libeskind, we wish to thank the Ministry of Foreign Affairs of the Federal Republic of Germany for underwriting the transportation of their models from Frankfurt and Berlin, and we thank Richard Zeisler for assisting us in enlisting the Ministry's support.

For the impetus to undertake this exhibition I must thank two men who are working on books related to our theme. First there is Aaron Betsky, who called my attention to the telling phrase "violated perfection"—originating from the title of an exhibition proposed by the team of Paul Florian and Stephen Wierzbowski for the University of Illinois, Chicago. The second man is Joseph Giovannini, who was another valuable source of preliminary information on the subject.

Special acknowledgment must go to Alvin Boyarsky and the Architectural Association of London, who acted as the key patron of most of the seven architects in their formative years. The A.A. has been the fertile soil from which many a new idea in architecture has sprouted.

I must thank the artists whose visions have moved me more even than any purely architectural drawings: Frank Stella, Michael Heizer, Ken Price, and Frank Gehry.

In the end, of course, the chief credit must be given to the seven architects and their teams, who not only produced the work, but prepared new drawings and models specially for the exhibition.

Philip Johnson
Curator of the Exhibition

Deconstructivist Architecture

Architecture has always been a central cultural institution valued above all for its provision of stability and order. These qualities are seen to arise from the geometric purity of its formal composition.

The architect has always dreamed of pure form, of producing objects from which all instability and disorder have been excluded. Buildings are constructed by taking simple geometric forms—cubes, cylinders, spheres, cones, pyramids, and so on—and combining them into stable ensembles (fig. 1), following compositional rules which prevent any one form from conflicting with another. No form is permitted to distort

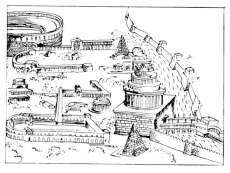

1

another; all potential conflict is resolved. The forms contribute harmoniously to a unified whole. This consonant geometric structure becomes the physical structure of the building: its formal purity is seen as guaranteeing structural stability.

Having produced this basic structure, the architect then elaborates it into a final design in a way that preserves its purity. Any deviation from the structural order, any impurity, is seen as threatening the formal values of harmony, unity, and stability, and is therefore insulated from the structure by being treated as mere ornament. Architecture is a conservative discipline that produces pure form and protects it from contamination.

The projects in this exhibition mark a different sensibility, one in which the dream of pure form has been disturbed. Form has become contaminated. The dream has become a kind of nightmare.

It is the ability to disturb our thinking about form that makes these projects deconstructive. It is not that they derive from the mode of contemporary philosophy known as "deconstruction."

They are not an application of deconstructive theory. Rather, they emerge from within the architectural tradition and happen to exhibit some deconstructive qualities.

Deconstruction itself, however, is often misunderstood as the taking apart of constructions.

3

Consequently, any provocative architectural design which appears to take structure apart—whether it be the simple breaking of an object (figs. 2, 3) or the complex dissimulation of an object into a collage of traces (figs. 4, 5)—has been hailed as deconstructive. These strategies have produced some of the most formidable projects of recent years, but remain simulations of deconstructive work in other disciplines, because they do not exploit the unique condition of the architectural object. Deconstruction is not

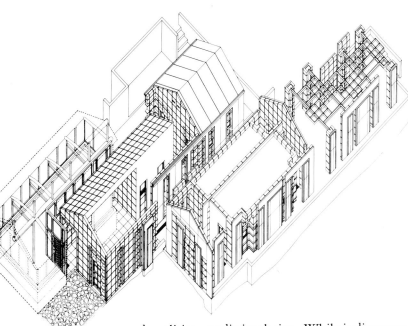

4

demolition, or dissimulation. While it diagnoses certain structural problems within apparently stable structures, these flaws do not lead to the structures' collapse. On the contrary, deconstruction gains all its force by challenging the very values of harmony, unity, and stability, and proposing instead a different view of structure: the view that the flaws are intrinsic to the structure.

They cannot be removed without destroying it; they are, indeed, structural.

A deconstructive architect is therefore not one who dismantles buildings, but one who locates the inherent dilemmas within buildings. The deconstructive architect puts the pure forms of the architectural tradition on the couch and identifies the symptoms of a repressed impurity. The impurity is drawn to the surface by a combination of gentle coaxing and violent torture: the form is interrogated.

To do so, each project employs formal strategies developed by the Russian avant-garde early in the twentieth century. Russian Constructivism constituted a critical turning point where the architectural tradition was bent so radically that a fissure opened up through which certain disturbing architectural possibilities first became visible. Traditional thinking about the nature of the

5

architectural object was placed in doubt. But the radical possibility was not then taken up. The wound in the tradition soon closed, leaving but a faint scar. These projects reopen the wound.

The Russian avant-garde posed a threat to tradition by breaking the classical rules of composition, in which the balanced, hierarchical relationship between forms creates a unified whole. Pure forms were now used to produce "impure," skewed, geometric compositions. Both the Supermatists, led by Malevich, and the constructors of three-dimensional works, primarily

Tatlin, placed simple forms in conflict to produce an unstable, restless geometry (figs. 6, 7). There was no single axis or hierarchy of forms but a nest of competing and conflicting axes and forms. In the years leading up to the 1917 revolution, this geometry became increasingly irregular.

In the years after the revolution, the avantgarde increasingly rejected the traditional high arts, as being an escape from social reality, but embraced architecture precisely because it is inherently functional and cannot be extracted from society. They saw architecture as a high art but one sufficiently grounded in function that it could be used to advance revolutionary goals; since architecture is so intertwined with society, the social revolution required an architectural revolution. Investigations began into using the pre-revolutionary art as the basis for radical structures. Having been lifted up out of the early drawings and into the counter-reliefs, the unstable geometric forms multiplied until they created a new kind of interior space (fig. 8) and seemed about to become architecture. Tatlin's monument (fig. 9), in which pure geometric forms become trapped in a twisted frame, seemed to announce a revolution in architecture. Indeed, for a few years a number of advanced designs were sketched. In Rodchenko's radio station (fig. 10), for example, the pure forms have broken through the structural frame, disturbing both it and themselves. In Krinskii's communal housing project (fig. 11), the frame has completely disintegrated; the forms no longer have any structural relationship and seem to have exploded from within.

But these radical structures were never realized. A critical shift in thinking took place. The more the Constructivists became committed to architecture, the more the instability of their pre-revolutionary work was removed. The conflict between forms, which defined the early work, was gradually resolved. Unstable assemblages of forms in conflict became machine-like assemblages of forms cooperating harmoniously in the achievement of specific goals. By the time of the canonic work of Constructivist architecture, the Vesnins' Palace of Labor, which was hailed as inaugurating a new age in architecture,

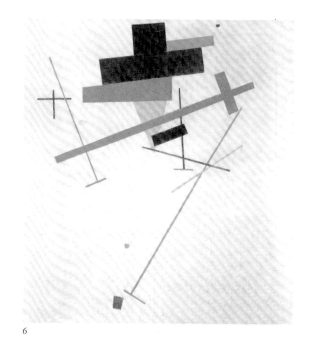

6

7

8

Fig. 6. *Kasimir Malevich. Suprematist Painting. 1915–16. Oil on canvas, 19¾ × 17½" (49 × 44.5 cm). Wilhelm-Hack-Museum, Ludwigshafen am Rhein, Federal Republic of Germany*

Fig. 7. *Vladimir Tatlin. Corner Counter-Relief. 1914–15. Iron, aluminum, zinc, paint. Whereabouts unknown*

Fig. 8. *Interior of the Café Pittoresque, Moscow, 1917. Decorations by Georgii Yakulov, Aleksandr Rodchenko, Vladimir Tatlin, and others*

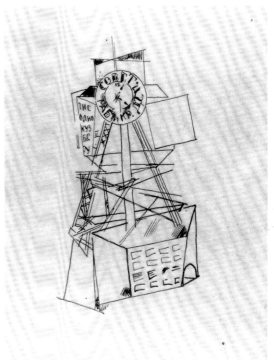

10

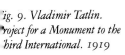

Fig. 9. Vladimir Tatlin.
Project for a Monument to the
Third International. 1919

Fig. 10. Aleksandr
Rodchenko. Experimental
design for a radio station.
1920

Fig. 11. Vladimir Krinskii.
Experimental design for communal housing. 1920

11

12

Fig. 12. Vesnin brothers.
Project for a Palace of Labor;
preliminary sketch for competition design. 1922–23

Fig. 13. Vesnin brothers.
Project for a Palace of Labor;
final scheme. 1923

Fig. 14. Aleksandr
Rodchenko. Design for a
newspaper kiosk. 1919

13

14

15

16

g. 15. Vladimir Tatlin.
aquette for stage set of
limir Khlebnikov's verse
ama Zangezi, performed
the Museum of Artistic
ulture, Petrograd, 1923

g. 16. Vladimir Tatlin.
aquette for stage set of
leksandr Ostrovsky's play
he Comic Actor of the
th Century, performed at
e Moscow Art Theater,
935

g. 17. Iakov Chernikhov.
onstructive Theatrical
et (illustration from his
ok The Construction of
rchitectural and Machine
orms, Leningrad, 1931)

the distinctive geometry of the early work is evident only in the overhead wires (fig. 12). And even then it is tamed further in the transition from the early sketch to the final design (fig. 13), changed from dangerous fantasy to safe reality. In the sketch the lines of the wires clash and the basic volumes are distorted. But in the final design the volumes have been purified—they have become smooth, classical—and the wires all converge in a single, hierarchical, vertical movement. All the tension of the early sketch is resolved into a single axis; the aimless geometry lines up. The project carries but a vestigial trace of the pre-revolutionary studies: the early work has become merely an ornament attached to the roof of a classical composition of pure forms. The structure below remains undisturbed.

Instability had been marginalized. Indeed, it was fully developed only in what had traditionally been considered marginal art forms— theater sets, street decorations, typography, photomontage, and clothing design (figs. 14–18)— arts exempt from the structural and functional constraints of building.

The Russian avant-garde were not prevented from building their early studies for simply political or technological reasons. Nor did they simply abandon the spirit of their early work. Rather, the instability of the pre-revolutionary work had never been proposed as a structural possibility. The early work was not concerned with destabilizing structure. On the contrary, it was concerned with the fundamental purity of structure. Its irregular geometry was understood as a dynamic relationship between forms floating in space rather than as an unstable structural condition intrinsic to the forms themselves. The purity of the individual forms was never called into question; their internal structure was never tampered with. But by attempting to turn the early formal experiments into contorted architectural structures, Tatlin, Rodchenko, and Krinskii transformed dynamism into instability. Their designs therefore constitute an aberration, an extreme possibility beyond the spirit of the early work. The more stable Constructivist architecture of the Vesnins, paradoxically, maintained that spirit, the concern with the purity of structure, precisely by protecting form from the threat of instability. And as a consequence, it was unable to disturb the traditional condition of the architectural object.

Architecture maintained its traditional role. In this sense, the radical avant-garde project failed in architecture. There are formal strategies possible in architecture which transform its fundamental condition; such transformations were effected in other arts, but not in architecture. There was only a stylistic shift, and even then the new style soon succumbed to that of the modern movement, which was developing in parallel at the same time. The Russian avant-garde was corrupted by the purity of the modern movement.

The modern movement attempted to purify architecture by stripping off the ornament of the classical tradition to reveal the naked purity of the functional structure beneath. Formal purity was associated with functional efficiency. But the modern movement was obsessed by an elegant aesthetic of functionalism, not by the complex dynamics of function itself. Rather than use the specific requirements of the functional program to generate the basic order of their projects, they merely manipulated the skin of pure geometric forms in a way that signified the general concept of function. By employing the machine aesthetic, they produced a functionalist style. Like the classicists, they articulated the surface of a form in a way that marked its purity. They restored the very tradition they attempted to escape, replacing the classical skin with a modern skin but not transforming the fundamental condition of the architectural object. Architecture remained an agent of stability.

Each of the projects in this exhibition explores the relationship between the instability of the early Russian avant-garde and the stability of high modernism. Each project employs the aesthetic of high modernism but marries it to the radical geometry of the pre-revolutionary work. They apply the cool veneer of the International Style to the anxiously conflicting forms of the avant-garde. Locating the tension of the early work under the skin of modern architecture, they irritate modernism from within, distorting it with its own genealogy.

It is not necessarily that they consciously work from Constructivist sources. Rather, in dismantling the ongoing tradition, in which modernism participated, they find themselves inevitably employing the strategies rehearsed by the avant-garde. They are not capriciously imitating the vocabulary of the Russians; the point is that the Russians discovered the geometric configurations which can be used to destabilize structure, and that these configurations can be found repressed within high modernism.

The use of the formal vocabulary of Constructivism is therefore not a historicist game which deftly extracts the avant-garde works from their ideologically charged social milieu by treating them as just aesthetic objects. The true aestheticization of the early formal investigations was actually effected when the avant-garde itself made them ornamental rather than structural. The projects in this exhibition, however, do make the early investigations structural, and thereby return them to the social milieu.

But this does not involve simply enlarging the counter-reliefs, or making the early drawings three-dimensional. These projects gain little of their force from employing conflicting forms. That merely sets the scene for a more fundamental subversion of the architectural tradition. The aesthetic is employed only in order to exploit a further radical possibility, one which the Russian avant-garde made available but did not take advantage of. If the projects in a sense complete the enterprise, in so doing they also transform it: they twist Constructivism. This twist is the "de" of "de-constructivist." The projects can be called deconstructivist because they draw from Constructivism and yet constitute a radical deviation from it.

They accomplish this by exploiting the aberration in the history of the avant-garde, the brief episode of about 1918–20 in which contorted architectural designs were proposed. Irregular geometry is again understood as a structural condition rather than as a dynamic formal aesthetic. It is no longer produced simply by the conflict between pure forms. It is now produced within those forms. The forms themselves are infiltrated with the characteristic skewed geometry, and distorted. In this way, the traditional condition of the architectural object is radically disturbed.

This disturbance does not result from an external violence. It is not a fracturing, or slicing, or fragmentation, or piercing. To disturb a form from the outside in these ways is not to threaten that form, only to damage it. The damage produces a decorative effect, an aesthetic of danger, an almost picturesque representation of peril — but not a tangible threat. Instead, deconstructivist architecture disturbs figures from within. But this does not mean that contorted geometry

Fig. 18. El Lissitzky. Untitled. 1924–30. Gelatin-silver print, 6¼ × 4⅝" (16.1 × 11.8 cm). The Museum of Modern Art, New York; Gift of Shirley C. Burden and David H. McAlpin (by exchange)

has become some new kind of interior decoration. It does not simply occupy the space defined by an already existing figure. The internal disturbance has actually been incorporated into the internal structure, the construction. It is as if some kind of parasite has infected the form and distorted it from the inside.

The rooftop remodeling project in this exhibition, for example (pls. 85–89), is clearly a form that has been distorted by some alien organism, a writhing, disruptive animal breaking through the corner. Some twisted counter-relief infects the orthogonal box. It is a skeletal monster which

18

breaks up the elements of the form as it struggles out. Released from the familiar constraints of orthogonal structure, the roof splits, shears, and buckles. The distortion is peculiarly disquieting because it seems to belong to the form, to be part of it. It seems to have always been latent there until released by the architect: the alien emerging out of the stairs, the walls, and the roof plane — not from some fissure or dark corner — is given shape by the very elements that define the basic volume of the attic. The alien is an outgrowth of the very form it violates.

The form is distorting itself. Yet this internal distortion does not destroy the form. In a strange way, the form somehow remains intact. This is an architecture of disruption, dislocation, deflection, deviation, and distortion, rather than one of demolition, dismantling, decay, decomposition, or disintegration. It displaces structure instead of destroying it.

What is finally so unsettling about such work is precisely that the form not only survives its torture, but appears all the stronger for it. Perhaps the form is even produced by it. It becomes unclear which came first, the form or the distortion, the host or the parasite. At first glance the difference between the form and its ornamental distortion appears clear, but on closer examination the line between them breaks up. The more carefully we look, the more unclear it becomes where the perfect form ends and its imperfection begins; they are found to be inseparably entangled. A line cannot be drawn between them. No surgical technique can free the form; no clean incision can be made. To remove the parasite would be to kill the host. They comprise one symbiotic entity.

This produces a feeling of unease, of disquiet, because it challenges the sense of stable, coherent identity that we associate with pure form. It is as if perfection had always harbored imperfection, that it has always had certain undiagnosed congenital flaws which are only now becoming visible. Perfection is secretly monstrous. Tortured from within, the seemingly perfect form confesses its crime, its imperfection.

This sense of dislocation occurs not only within the forms of these projects. It also occurs between those forms and their context.

In recent years, the modern understanding of social responsibility as functional program has been superseded by a concern for context. But contextualism has been used as an excuse for mediocrity, for a dumb servility to the familiar. Since deconstructivist architecture seeks the unfamiliar within the familiar, it displaces the context rather than acquiesce to it. The projects in this exhibition do not ignore the context; they are not anti-contextual. Rather, each makes a very specific intervention.

What makes them disturbing is the way they find the unfamiliar already hidden within the familiar context. By their intervention, elements of the context become defamiliarized. In one project, towers are turned over on their sides, while in others, bridges are tilted up to become towers, underground elements erupt from the earth and float above the surface, or commonplace materials become suddenly exotic. Each project activates some part of the context to disturb the rest of it, drawing out previously unnoticed disruptive properties and making them thematic. Each thereby assumes an uncanny presence, alien to the context from which it derives, strange yet familiar—a kind of sleeping monster which awakens in the midst of the everyday.

This estrangement sets up a complicated resonance, between the disrupted interior of the forms and their disruption of the context, which calls into question the status of the walls that define the form. The division between inside and outside is radically disturbed. The form no longer simply divides an inside from an outside. The geometry proves to be much more convoluted: the sense of being enclosed, whether by a building or a room, is disrupted. But not by simply removing walls—the closure of form is not simply replaced by the openness of the modern free plan. This is not freedom, liberation, but stress; not release, but greater tension. The wall breaks open, and in a very ambiguous way. There are no simple windows, no regular openings puncturing a solid wall; rather, the wall is tormented—split and folded. It no longer provides security by dividing the familiar from the unfamiliar, inside from out. The whole condition of enclosure breaks down.

Even though it threatens this most fundamental property of architectural objects, deconstructivist architecture does not constitute an avant-garde. It is not a rhetoric of the new. Rather, it exposes the unfamiliar hidden within the traditional. It is the shock of the old.

It exploits the weaknesses in the tradition in order to disturb rather than overthrow it. Like the modern avant-garde, it attempts to be disturbing, alienating. But not from the retreat of the avant-garde, not from the margins. Rather, it occupies, and subverts, the center. This work is not fundamentally different from the ancient tradition it subverts. It does not abandon the tradition. Rather, it inhabits the center of the tradition in order to demonstrate that architecture is always infected, that pure form has always

been contaminated. By inhabiting the tradition fully, obeying its inner logic more rigorously than ever before, these architects discover certain dilemmas within the tradition that are missed by those who sleepwalk through it.

Deconstructivist architecture therefore poses problems to both the center and the margins, both the conservative mainstream and the radical fringe of the architectural profession. Neither can simply appropriate the work. It cannot simply be imitated by the margins, because it demands such an intimate knowledge of, and therefore complicity with, the inner workings of the tradition. But neither can it simply be appropriated by the center; it cannot be so easily assimilated. It invites consumption by employing traditional architectural forms—tempts the profession to swallow it whole—but, because it infects those forms, it always produces a kind of indigestion. In that moment of critical resistance it assumes its full force.

Much supposedly radical architectural work of recent years has neutralized itself by maintaining itself in the margins. A body of brilliant conceptual projects has developed which perhaps look more radical than the work in this exhibition but lack its force, because they do not confront the center of the tradition: they marginalize themselves by excluding building. They do not engage with architecture but make sophisticated glosses on it. They produce a kind of commentary on building without entering into building. Such drawings have written into them the detachment of the historical avant-garde. They inhabit the margins, the ones up front, at the frontier. They are projections of the future, brave new worlds, utopian fantasies.

In contrast, the work in this exhibition is neither a projection into the future nor simply a historicist remembrance of the past. Rather, it attempts to get under the skin of the living tradition, irritating it from within. Deconstructivist architecture locates the frontiers, the limits of architecture, coiled up within everyday forms. It finds new territory within old objects.

This work carries out the kind of subversion usually regarded as possible only in realms distanced from the reality of built form. The projects are radical precisely because they do not play in the sanctuaries of drawing, or theory, or sculpture. They inhabit the realm of building. Some have been built, some will be built, and others will never be built—but each is buildable; each aims at building. They develop an architectonic coherence by confronting the basic problems of building—structure and function—even if they do so in an unconventional way.

In each project, the traditional structure of parallel planes—stacked up horizontally from the ground plane within a regular form—is twisted. The frame is warped. Even the ground plane is warped. The interrogation of pure form pushes structure to its limits, but not beyond. The structure is shaken but does not collapse; it is just pushed to where it becomes unsettling. The work produces a sense of unease when floors and walls move disconcertingly, tempting us to trust something closer to the edge. But if these structures produce a sense of insecurity, it is not because of flimsiness. These buildings are extremely solid. The solidity is just organized in an unfamiliar way, shifting our traditional sense of structure. Though structurally sound, at the same time they are structurally frightening.

This displacement of traditional thinking about structure also displaces traditional thinking about function. The modernists argued that form follows function, and that functionally efficient forms necessarily had a pure geometry. But their streamlined aesthetic disregarded the untidy reality of actual functional requirements. In deconstructivist architecture, however, the disruption of pure form provides a dynamic complexity of local conditions that is more congruent with functional complexity. Moreover, forms are disturbed and only then given a functional program. Instead of form following function, function follows deformation.

Despite calling into question traditional ideas about structure, these projects are rigorously structural. Despite calling into question the functionalist rhetoric of modernism, each project is rigorously functional.

For most of the architects, this commitment to building is a recent shift that has completely changed the tone of their work. They have left their complex abstractions and confronted the materiality of built objects. This shift gives their work a critical edge. Critical work today can be done only in the realm of building: to engage with the discourse, architects have to engage with building; the object becomes the site of all theoretical inquiry. Theorists are forced out of

the sanctuary of theory, practitioners are roused from sleepwalking practice. Both meet in the realm of building, and engage with objects.

This should not be understood as a rejection of theory. Rather, it indicates that the traditional status of theory has changed. No longer is it some abstract realm of defense that surrounds objects, protecting them from examination by mystifying them. Architectural theory generally preempts an encounter with the object. It is concerned with veiling rather than exposing objects. With these projects, all the theory is loaded into the object: propositions now take the form of objects rather than verbal abstractions. What counts is the condition of the object, not the abstract theory. Indeed the force of the object makes the theory that produced it irrelevant.

Consequently, these projects can be considered outside their usual theoretical context. They can be analyzed in strictly formal terms because the formal condition of each object carries its full ideological force. Such an analysis brings together highly conceptual architects with pragmatists. They join together in the production of disquieting objects which interrogate pure form, in a way that exposes the repressed condition of architecture.

This is not to say that they participate in a new movement. Deconstructivist architecture is not an "-ism." But neither is it simply seven independent architects. It is a curious point of intersection among strikingly different architects moving in different directions. The projects are but brief moments in the independent programs of the artists. Clearly, they influence each other in complex ways, but this is not a team; it is, at best, an uneasy alliance. This exhibition is as much about the uneasiness as it is about an alliance. The episode will be short-lived. The architects will proceed in different directions. Their work will not authorize a certain kind of practice, a certain kind of object. This is not a new style; the projects do not simply share an aesthetic. What the architects share is the fact that each constructs an unsettling building by exploiting the hidden potential of modernism.

The disquiet these buildings produce is not merely perceptual; it is not a personal response to the work, nor even a state of mind. What is being disturbed is a set of deeply entrenched cultural assumptions which underlie a certain view of architecture, assumptions about order, harmony, stability, and unity. Yet this disturbance does not derive from, or result in, some fundamental shift in culture. The disquiet is not produced by some new spirit of the age; it is not that an unsettled world produces an unsettled architecture. It is not even the personal angst of the architect; it is not a form of expressionism— the architect expresses nothing here. The architect only makes it possible for the tradition to go wrong, to deform itself. The nightmare of deconstructivist architecture inhabits the unconscious of pure form rather than the unconscious of the architect. The architect merely countermands traditional formal inhibitions in order to release the suppressed alien. Each architect releases different inhibitions in order to subvert form in radically different ways. Each makes thematic a different dilemma of pure form.

In so doing they produce a devious architecture, a slippery architecture that slides uncontrollably from the familiar into the unfamiliar, toward an uncanny realization of its own alien nature: an architecture, finally, in which form distorts itself in order to reveal itself anew. The projects suggest that architecture has always been riddled with these kinds of enigmas, that they are the source of its force and its delight—that they are the very possibility of its formidable presence.

Mark Wigley
Associate Curator of the Exhibition

PROJECTS

Frank O. Gehry

Frank O. Gehry and Associates, Inc.

Born in Toronto, Canada, 1929
Based in Venice, California

Gehry House. Santa Monica, California. 1978–88
First Stage. 1978
    Associate: Paul Lubowicki
Second Stage. 1979
    Associate: Paul Lubowicki
Third Stage. 1988
    Associate: Susan Narduli

Familian House. Santa Monica, California. 1978
    Associates: John Clagett, C. Gregory Walsh

The Gehry house is a renovation, in three stages, of an existing suburban building. The original house is now embedded in several interlocking additions of conflicting structures. It has been severely distorted by those additions. But the force of the house comes from the sense that the additions were not imported to the site but emerged from the inside of the house. It is as if the house had always harbored these twisted shapes within it.

In the first stage (pls. 2–5), forms twist their way out from the inside. A tilted cube (pl. 3), for example, made up of the timber framing of the original house, bursts through the structure, peeling back the layers of the house. As these forms push their way out, they lift off the skin of the building, exposing the structure; they create a second skin which wraps around the front and sides of the new volume, but which peels right off the rear wall of the house to stand free, like stage scenery. Having broken through the structure, the forms strain against this second skin, but in the end it stops them from escaping. Consequently, the first stage operates in the gap between the original wall and its displaced skin. This gap is a zone of conflict in which stable distinctions, between inside and out, original and addition, structure and facade, are questioned. The original house becomes a strange artifact, trapped and distorted by forms that have emerged from within it.

In the second stage (pls. 6–9), the structure of the rear wall, which is unprotected by the skin, bursts and planks tumble out. The structure almost literally breaks down. In the third stage (pls. 1, 10–12), the backyard fills up with forms that appear to have escaped from the house through the breach in the rear wall, which then closes. These forms are then put under tension by being twisted relative to each other and to the house. The Gehry house becomes an extended essay on the convoluted relationship between the conflict within forms and the conflict between forms.

The Familian house (pls. 13–21) is composed of a cube and a bar. Within the cube, a smaller cube twists and turns. As a result of this internal conflict, the smaller cube breaks up within the larger one, its bottom face remaining as a floor plane suspended within the larger cube while the rest corkscrews its way out through the roof and tilts back (pl. 20). This diagonal twisting within the cube also throws out a bridge, which leaps out horizontally, through the skin, and across the gap between the two forms, bonding them together.

Both the cube and the bar are disturbed, but in different ways. The end wall of the bar is dismembered and slides out to form the balcony (pl. 15), its elements twisting vertically and horizontally in the process. But unlike the breakdown of the small cube, this is not one form subverting another from within. The internal volume of the bar is not disturbed. All the tension is in the walls that define that volume. The walls are placed under sufficient stress that gashes open up: the pure white modernist skin tears, and peels off, exposing an unexpectedly contorted timber frame. Pure form is interrogated in a way that reveals its twisted and splintered structure.

Gehry House
1. (Overleaf) Model, third
stage
2. Axonometric, first stage
3—5. Model, first stage

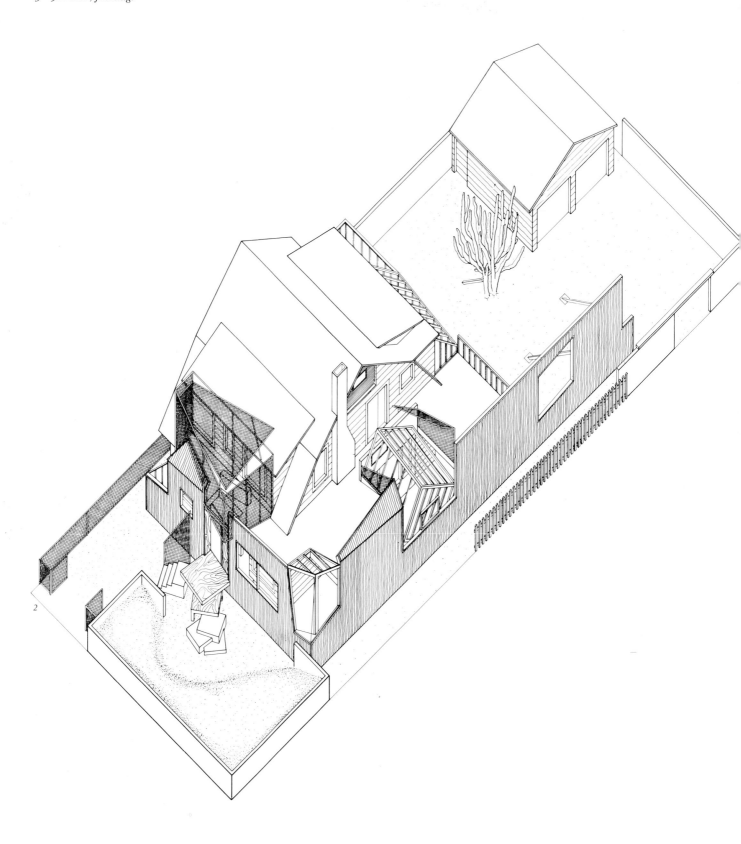

2

4

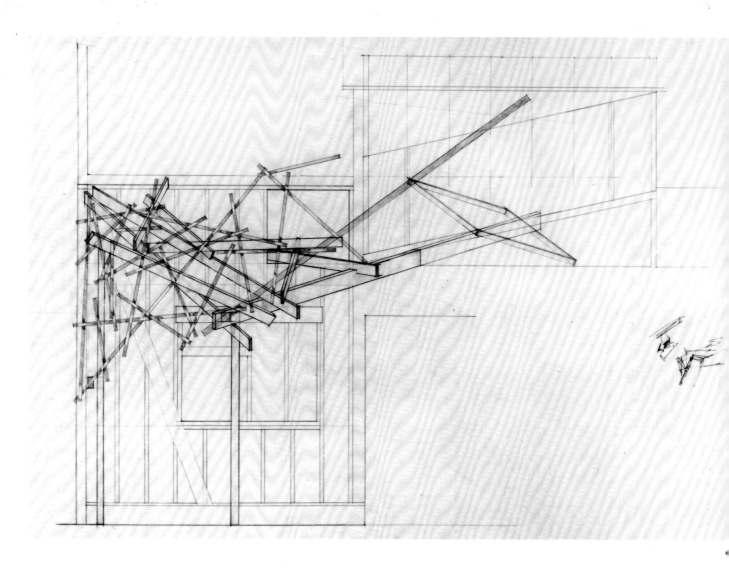

6. Elevation, second stage
7, 8. Model, second stage
9. Detail of model, second
stage; bird's-eye view

7

10

11

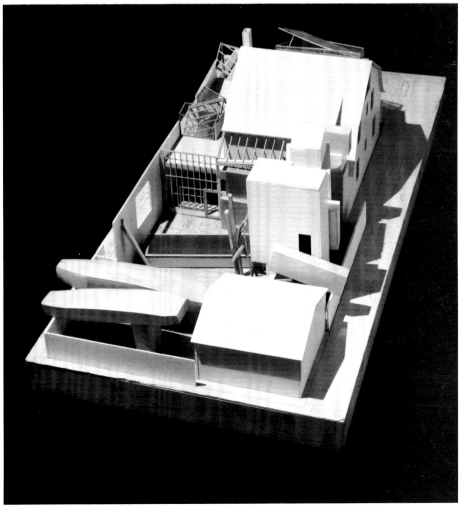

11–12. Model, third stage

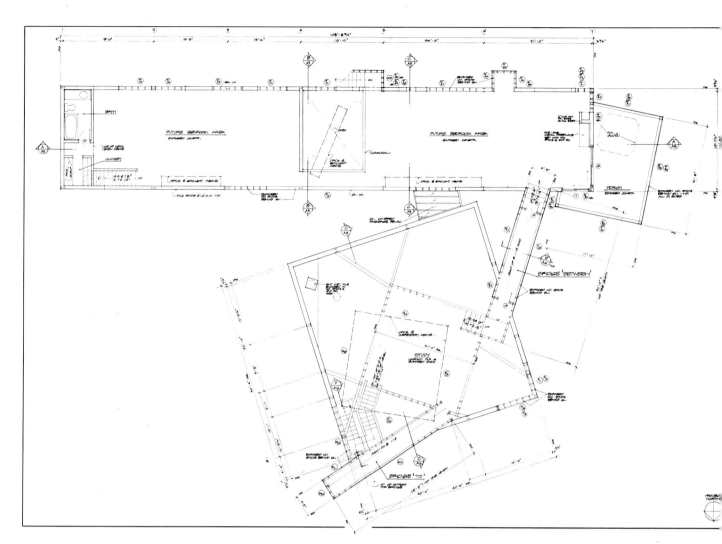

15

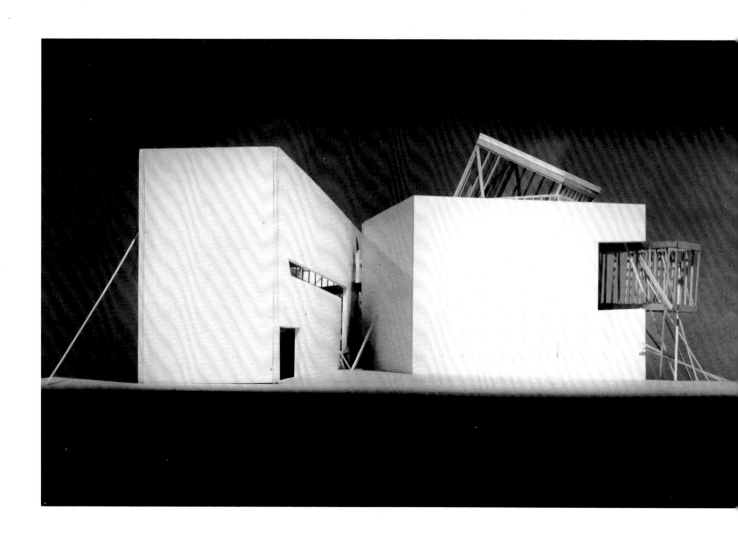

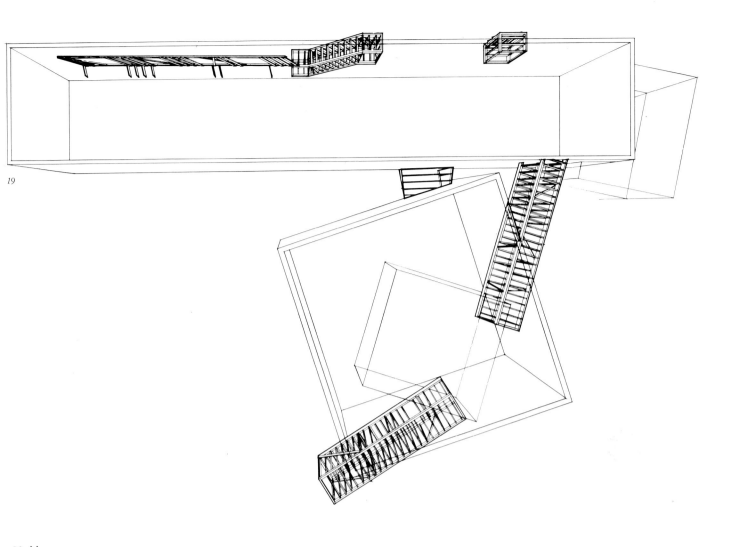

19

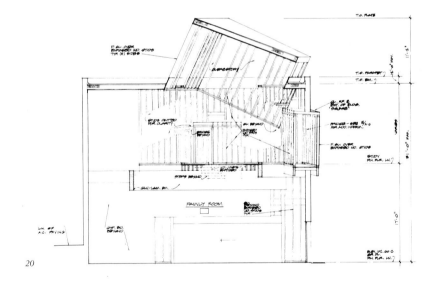

20

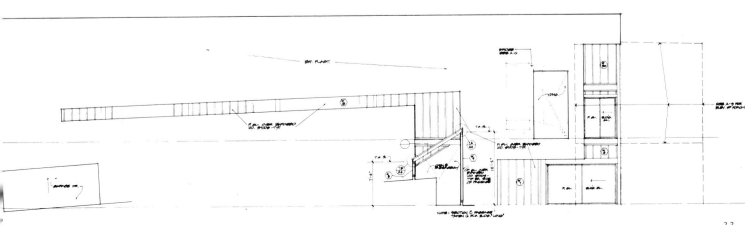

Daniel Libeskind

Born in Lodz, Poland, 1946
Based in Milan, Italy

City Edge. Berlin, Federal Republic of Germany.
1987
Awarded First Prize, IBA City Edge Competition. 1987
Assistants: Donald L. Bates, Meton Gadelha, Thomas Han, Dean Hoffman, Juha Ilonen, Esbjorn Jonsson, Brian Nicholson, Hani Rashid, Berit Restad-Jonsson, Lars Henrik Stahl, Joseph Wong
Structural Engineer: Peter Rice (Ove Arup and Partners)

The City Edge project is an office and residential development for the Tiergarten district of Berlin. It is a colossal bar angled up from the ground so that one end floats ten stories high, looking over the Berlin Wall.

The project exploits the logic of that wall, the violent slicing up of territory. The bar is an abstraction of the wall, slicing through the city, breaking fragments off the old city structure. But then it subverts the logic of the wall by lifting itself up and creating a new public street below: it becomes a device for breaking down divisions rather than establishing them.

The wall is further transformed by being broken into pieces, which are then twisted against each other. At one end of the site, a pile of smaller, solid bars is assembled; at the other, the main bar competes against its shadow, which is cut into the ground (pl. 32). The wall is thus made to cross over itself many times in ways that conflict with its ability to simply define enclosure.

By dismembering the wall, traditional thinking about structure is also broken down. The rational, orderly grid (pl. 27) actually turns out to be made up of a series of decentered spaces, which are cut by aimless, folded lines and inhabited by a scattering of small squares that have been dislodged from the orthogonal structure. This becomes a new reading of the disorder within the city itself, a reading disclosed when the authority of the walls that define its structure is undermined.

The symbolic breakdown of the wall effected by introducing the Constructivist motifs of tilted and crossed bars sets up a subversion of the walls that define the bar itself. Inside, the bar is a jumble of folded planes, crossed forms, counter-reliefs, spinning movements, and contorted shapes (pl. 28). This apparent chaos actually constructs the walls that define the bar; it is the structure. The internal disorder produces the bar even while splitting it, even as gashes open up along its length (pl. 25).

The apparently neutral surface of the perfect bar is not, therefore, a skin holding in a chaotic world. It is actually constructed, like a quilt, out of fragments of that world (pl. 33). The surface is not a neutral screen which divides the internal contorted geometry of the bar from the external contorted geometry of the city: it is a side effect of their dialogue. Each of the models explores a different aspect of this dialogue. They set up a convoluted geometry between the twisted forms that inhabit the bar and the disorder of the city that the bar exploits. They obey the logic of the city precisely in order to disturb the city. In this way, the project engages the city while remaining estranged from it.

35

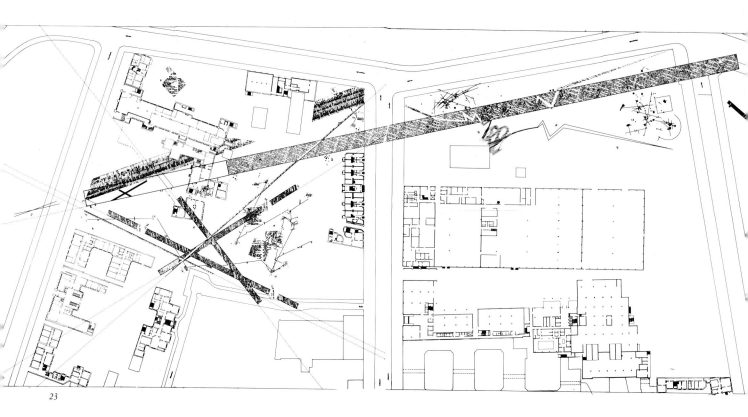

23

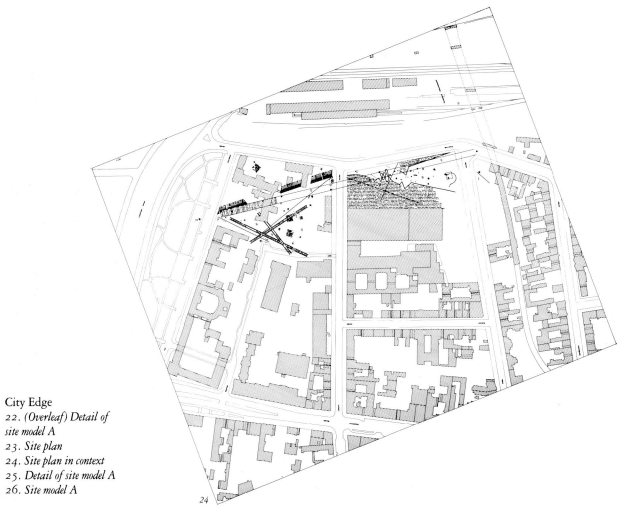

City Edge
22. (Overleaf) Detail of
site model A
23. Site plan
24. Site plan in context
25. Detail of site model A
26. Site model A

24

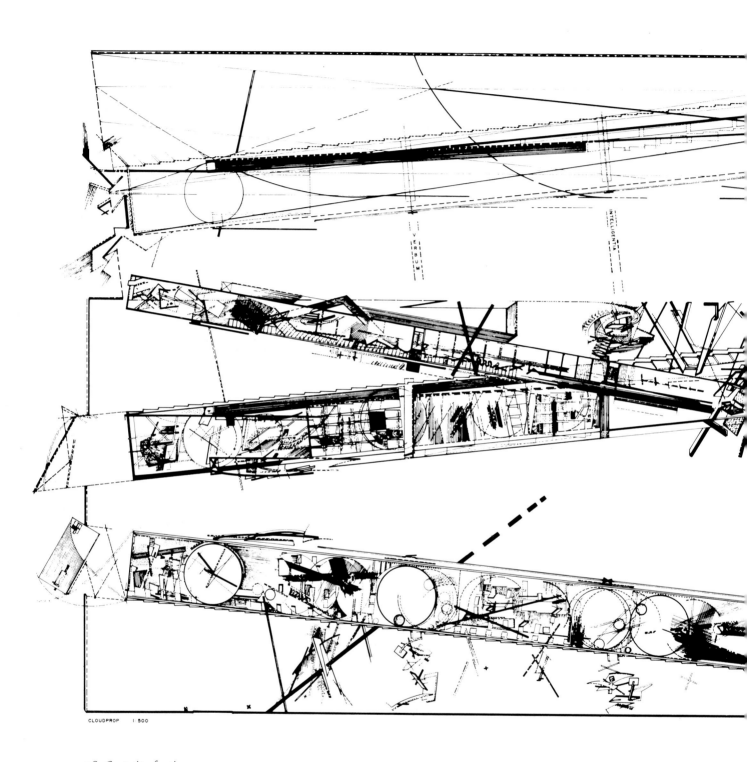

CLOUDPROP 1:500

28. *Composite of sections*

40

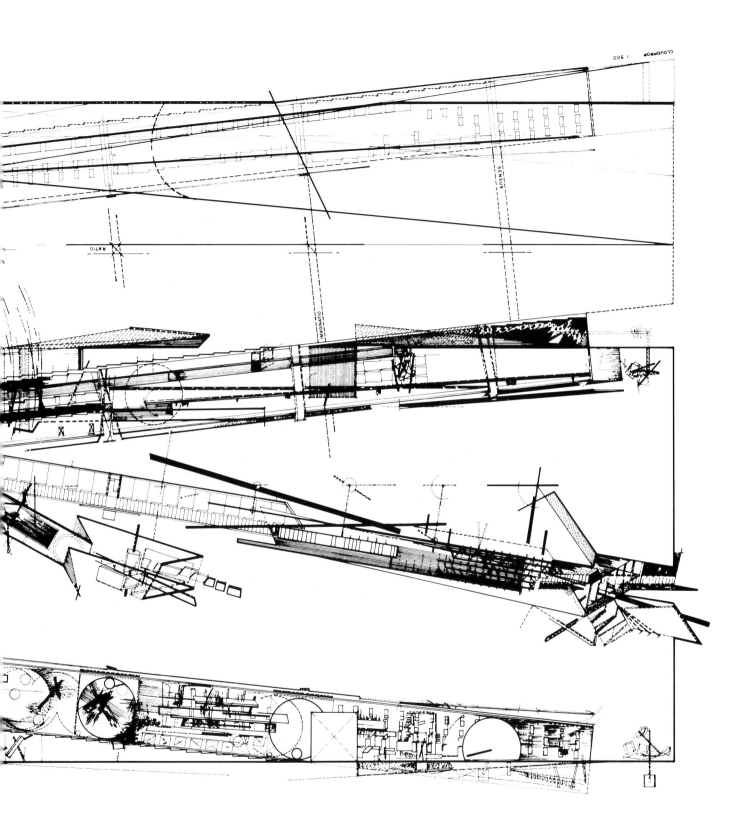

CLOUDPROP 1:500

RATIO

SENSUS

IMAGNATIO

41

29. Sections and exploded
axonometric of structure and
circulation
30, 31. Sectional model,
two views

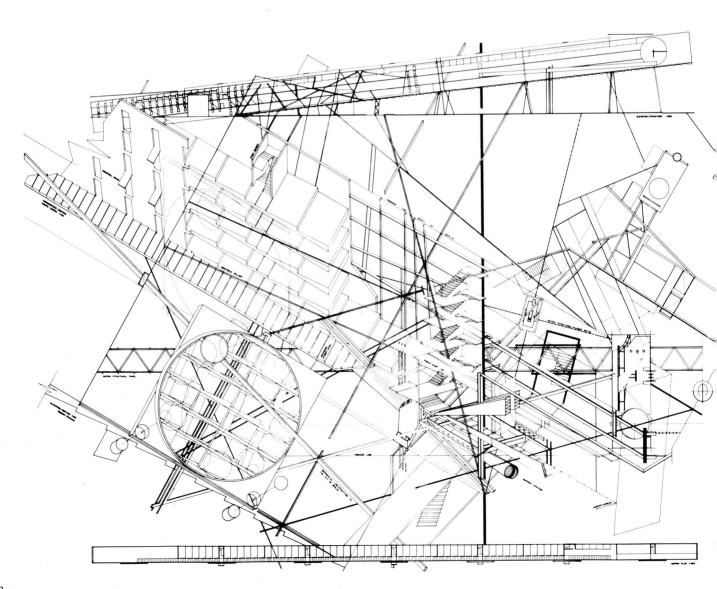

*. Site model B
*, 34. Hanging model,
o views

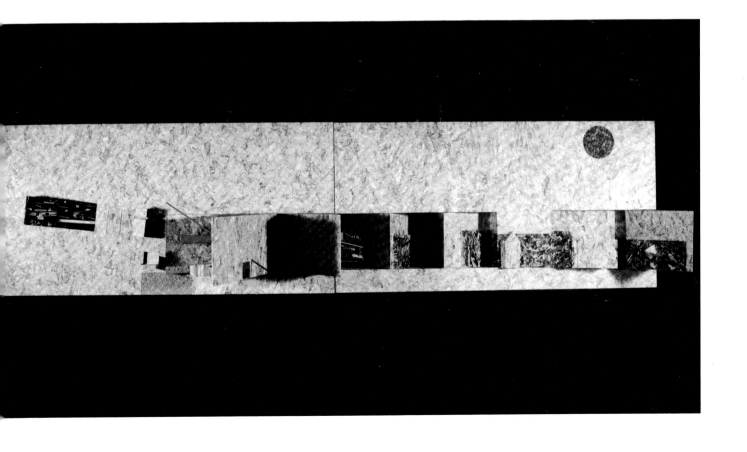

Rem Koolhaas
Office for Metropolitan Architecture

Born in Rotterdam, Holland, 1944
Based in Rotterdam, Holland

Apartment Building and Observation Tower.
   Rotterdam, Holland. 1982
Associates: Stefano de Martino, Kees Christiaanse

The Rotterdam project is a high-rise apartment building whose base contains communal facilities, such as a kindergarten and school, and whose top forms a street in the sky along which is a hotel, with club, health center, and swimming pool. It is located on a narrow headland between the Maas River and a parallel canal, a kind of no-man's-land cut off from the city and traversed by a major road (pl. 36).

The building is enigmatically poised between being essentially a single slab, a homogeneous monolith (like its neighbors), but distorted by a number of towers, and being essentially a row of discrete towers, distorted by a slab. From the river (pl. 40), it appears as a row of solid towers against a glass horizon; from the city (pl. 39), as a stone slab with glass towers attached to it.

The struggle between towers and slab opens up gaps, either as a narrow slit, a huge hole in the volume, or a complete void. Whenever these gaps appear, whenever the skin is pulled back or the volumes are punctured, a system of floating floor planes is exposed. Throughout, strong horizontal lines act as a datum against which the slab and towers play. Everything shifts, except those lines: each surface, each section, each plan is different. Tension even develops between the towers, in addition to that between the slab and the towers. Each of the towers has a different angle to the slab: some fall backwards, others are contained, others twist away, while some have broken free.

At one end of the slab, a pure orthogonal tower begins to detach itself (pl. 35). At the other end, an angled open-steel tower has escaped altogether (pl. 44). It is produced by taking a section of an old bridge on the site and lifting it up to form a tilted tower (pl. 41). Suspended between the two—the high-modernist tower and the angular Constructivist tower—the slab becomes the scene of a radical questioning of modernism. It is seen to give birth to both the stability of the one and the instability of the other. But the status of the slab is thrown even further in doubt because both of the towers related to it emerge as much from the context as from the slab itself. The identity of modernism becomes elusive; its limits are no longer clear.

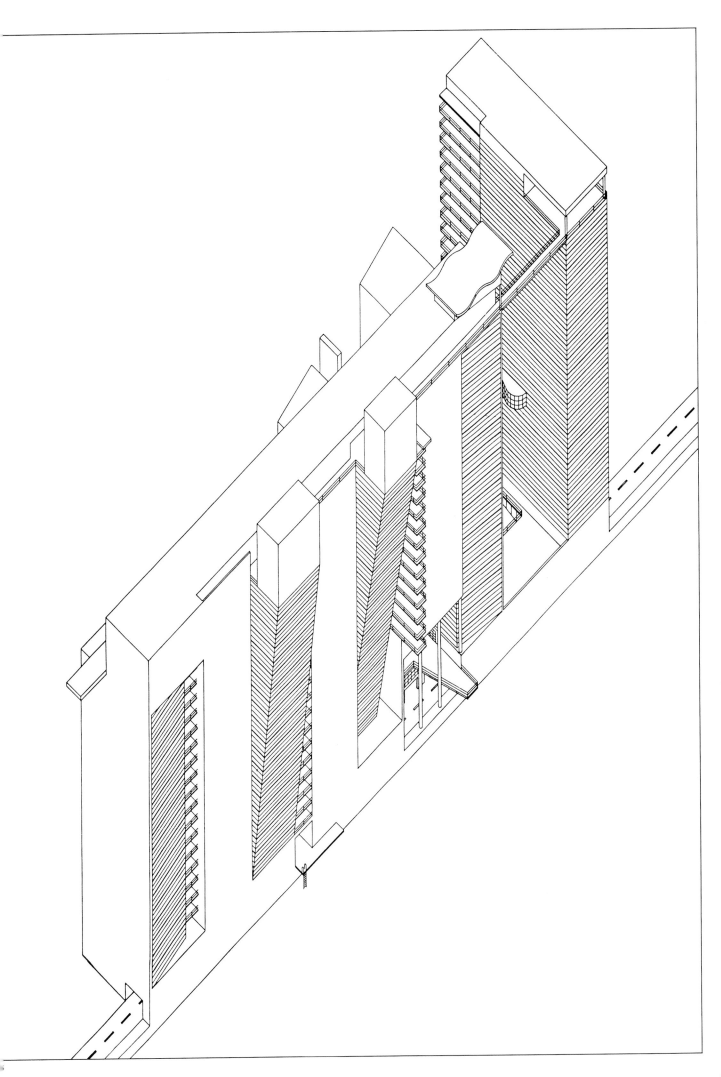

47

Apartment Building and
Observation Tower
*35. (Overleaf) Axonometric
from city side
36. Isometric triptych:*
Rotterdam Summation.
1982

36

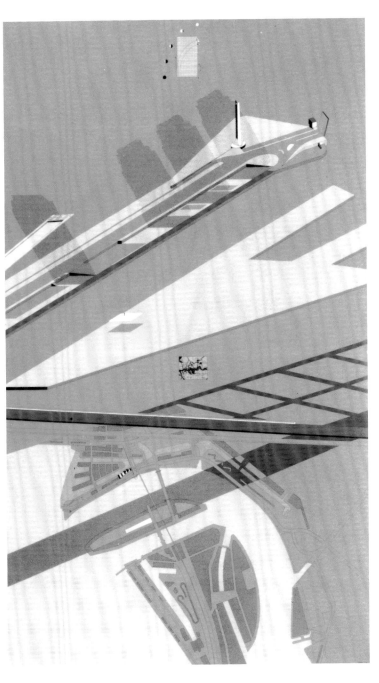

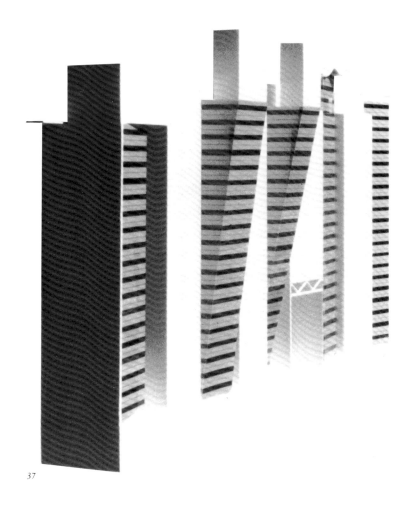

37

37. *Final model*
38. *Study model*
39. *Axonometric from city side*
40. *Axonometric from river side*

38

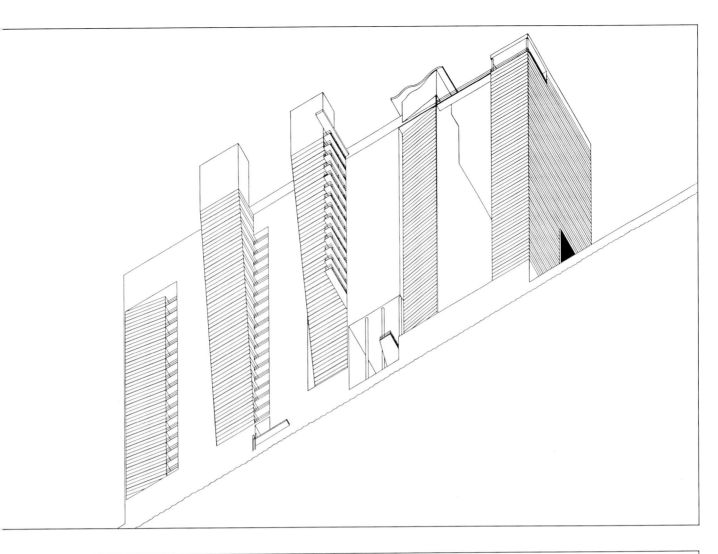

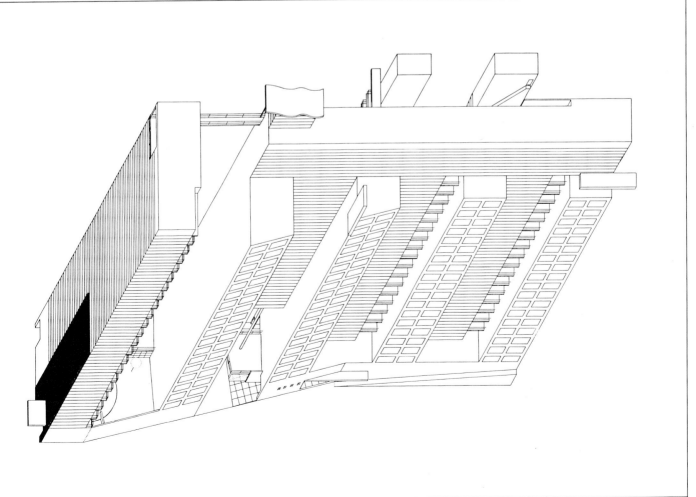

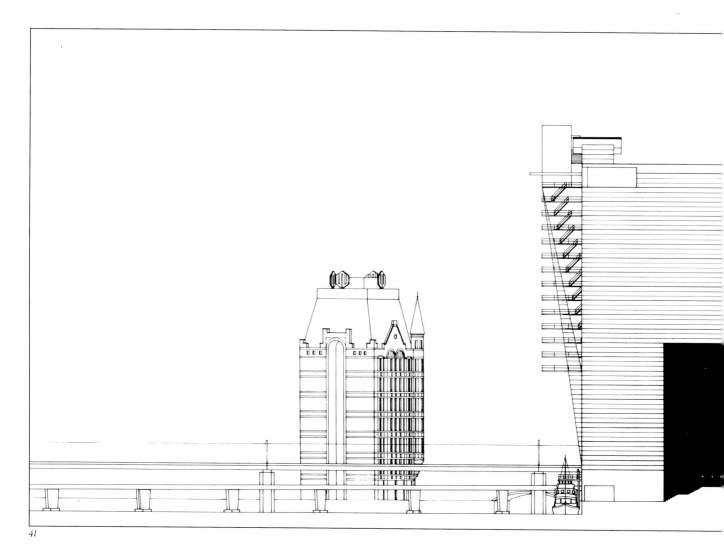

41

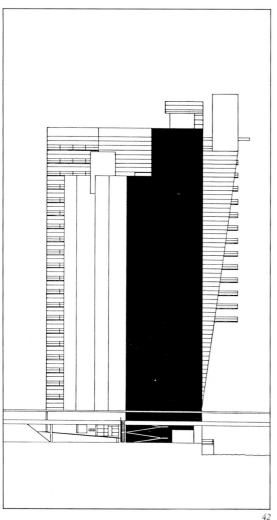

42

41. *West elevation of building and tower in context*
42. *East elevation*
43. *Perspective from river side*

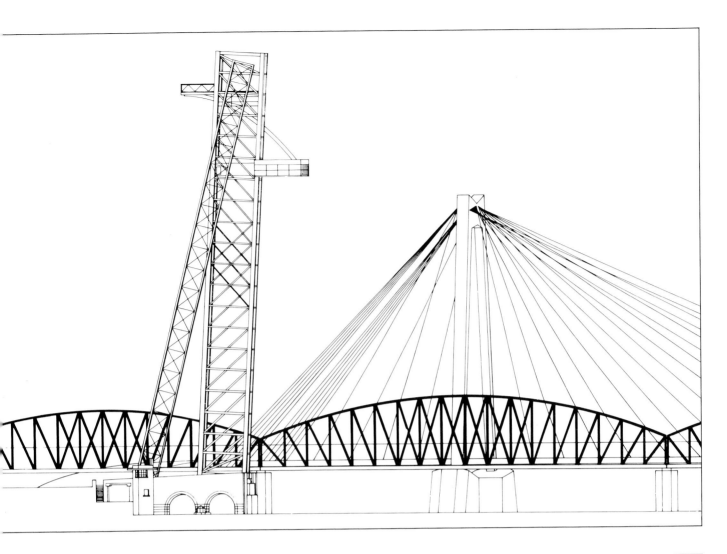

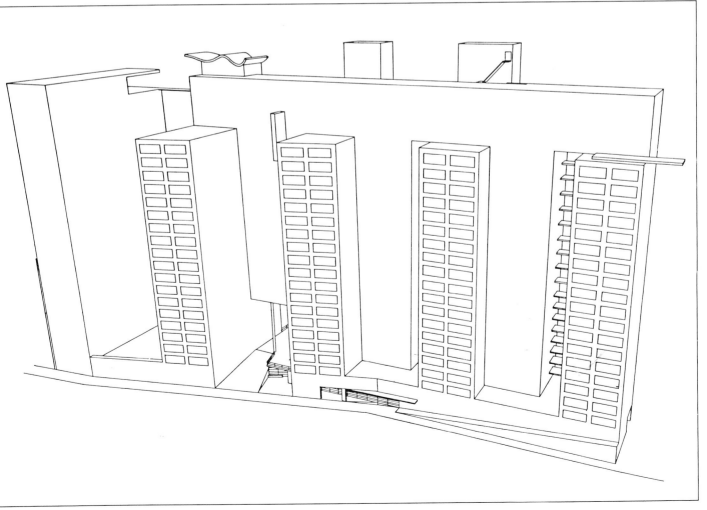

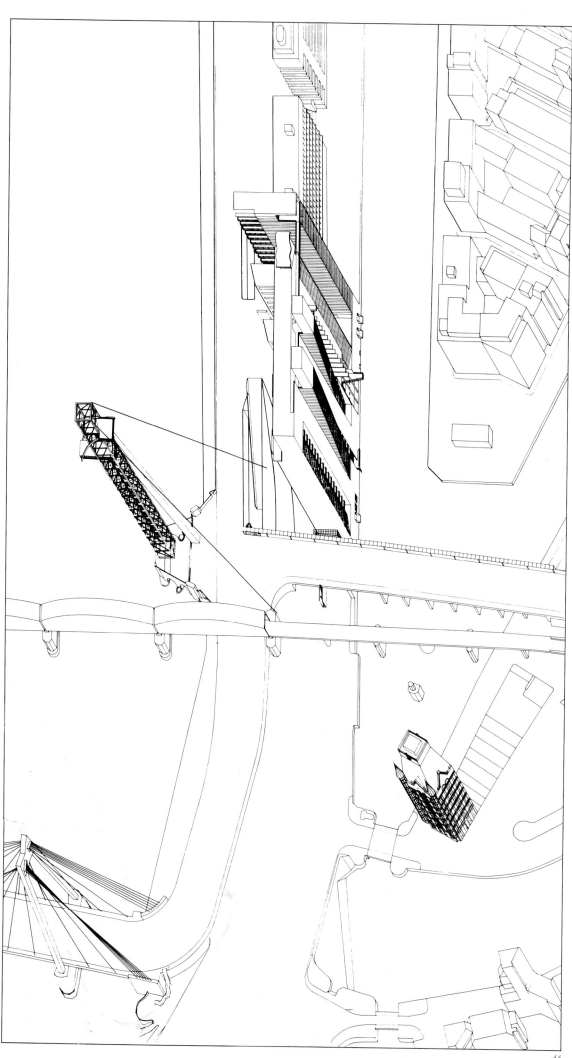

44. *Axonometric of buildi*
and tower in context
45. *Axonometric of tower*

Peter Eisenman
Eisenman Robertson Architects

Born in Newark, New Jersey, 1932
Based in New York, New York

Biocenter for the University of Frankfurt.
    Frankfurt am Main, Federal Republic of
    Germany. 1987
Awarded Special Prize, Biocenter International
    Competition. 1987
Associate: Thomas Leeser
Artist: Michael Heizer
Project Team: Hiroshi Maruyama, David Biagi,
    Sylvain Boulanger, Ken Doyno, Judy Geib,
    Holger Kleine, Christian Kohl, Greg Lynn,
    Carlene Ramus, Wolfgang Rettenmaier,
    Madison Spencer, Paul Sorum, Sarah Whit-
    ing, David Youse
Mechanical Engineer: Augustine DiGiacomo
    (Jaros, Baum and Bolles)
Structural Engineer: Robert Silman
    (Silman Associates)
Landscape Architect: Laurie Olin
    (Hanna-Olin)
Color Consultant: Robert Slutzky

This project is a center for advanced biological research for the University of Frankfurt. It is based on a symmetrical distribution of laboratory units along a spine. The spine (pl. 55) is a single extruded space—a long, transparent bar traversed by bridges—which acts as the central circulation and social space.

The units spread out along this spine are basic modernist blocks, rational units organized by a rational system. Each one is given the form of one of the four basic shapes which biologists use as a code to describe fundamental biological processes (pl. 47). The biologists' graphic code takes on architectural form, becoming the very structure of the project. But this intersection of modernist abstraction and an arbitrary figurative code, which acts as the basic form, is then progressively distorted to provide the functionally specific social and technical spaces. The distortion is effected by systematically adding further shapes in a way that clashes—new shapes that come out of the same system of four basic shapes that they distort. They are added to the basic form—both as solids in space and as voids cut into the ground—in a way that calls its configuration into question, disturbing both the forms (pl. 49) and the spine that organizes them (pl. 48).

The result is a complex dialogue between the basic form and its distortions. A world of unstable forms emerges from within the stable structures of modernism. And those multiplying forms clash in ways that create a range of relationships: sometimes there is no conflict, as one form passes over or under another; sometimes one form is simply embedded within another; sometimes one form eats into another; sometimes both forms are disturbed and a new form is produced. The project becomes a complex exchange between solid, void, and transparency.

This project also engages the context, by exploiting the angle of an underground service core already on the site. The angle is used to organize the building, but also to disturb it. Below ground, it fractures the very building it services (pl. 56); above ground, it becomes a service road that is in turn broken by the building (pl. 59). This leaves the status of both unclear.

The same convoluted relationship exists between the building and Michael Heizer's *Dragged Mass No. 3*, a huge, abstracted rock which is dragged through the site, leaving a polished gash (pls. 50–54). The mass undercuts the building, only to be stopped by an abstracted pile of spoil, through which the architect's road cuts. A close collaboration between artist and architect here takes the form of a duel: each operates on the same scale; each scars the other. Art is no longer something that is given a segregated space in an architectural project, nor something absorbed by it. Rather, art and architecture compete on equal terms: each contributes to the form of the other even while distorting it. Between them, the traditional opposition of abstraction and figuration is undermined. It is no longer possible to separate structural work from ornamental play.

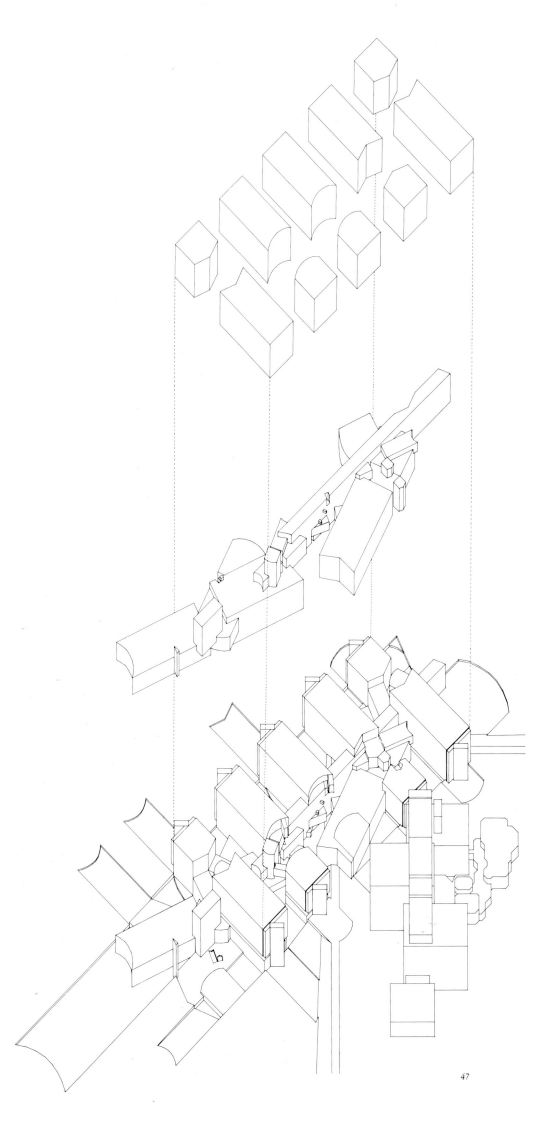

Biocenter
46. *(Overleaf) Site model*
47. *Exploded axonometric.*
basic units, spine, and over
all mass
48. *Study model of spine*
49. *Study model of mass*

47

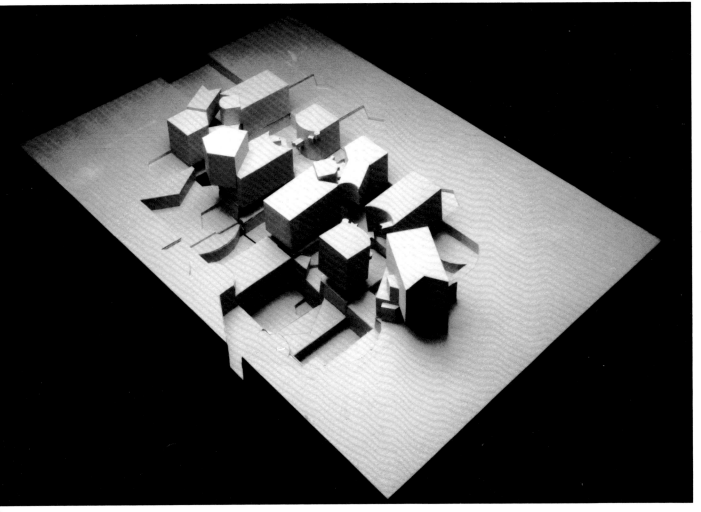

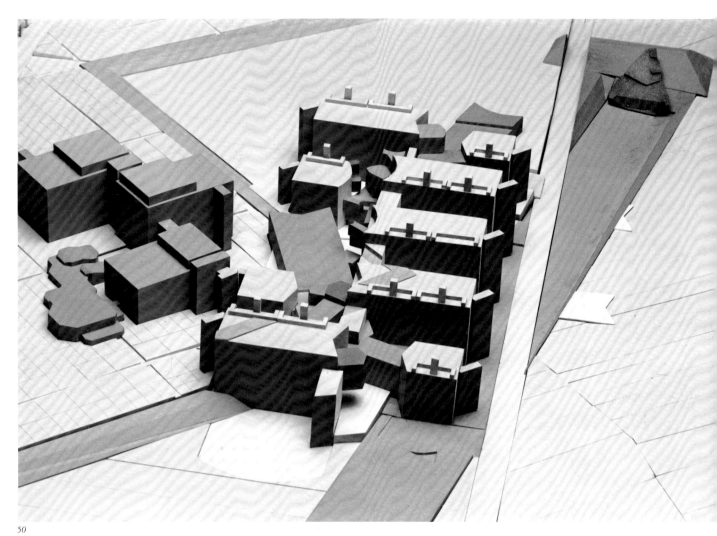

50

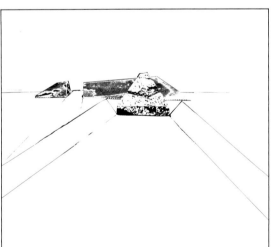

51

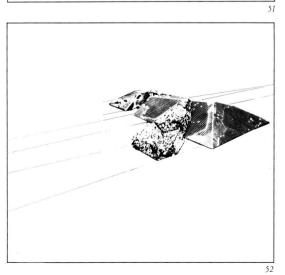

52

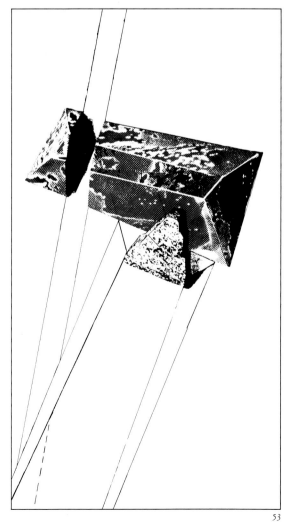

53

50. Site model B
51–53. Michael Heizer.
Studies for model of
Dragged Mass No. 3.
1987
54. Site plan

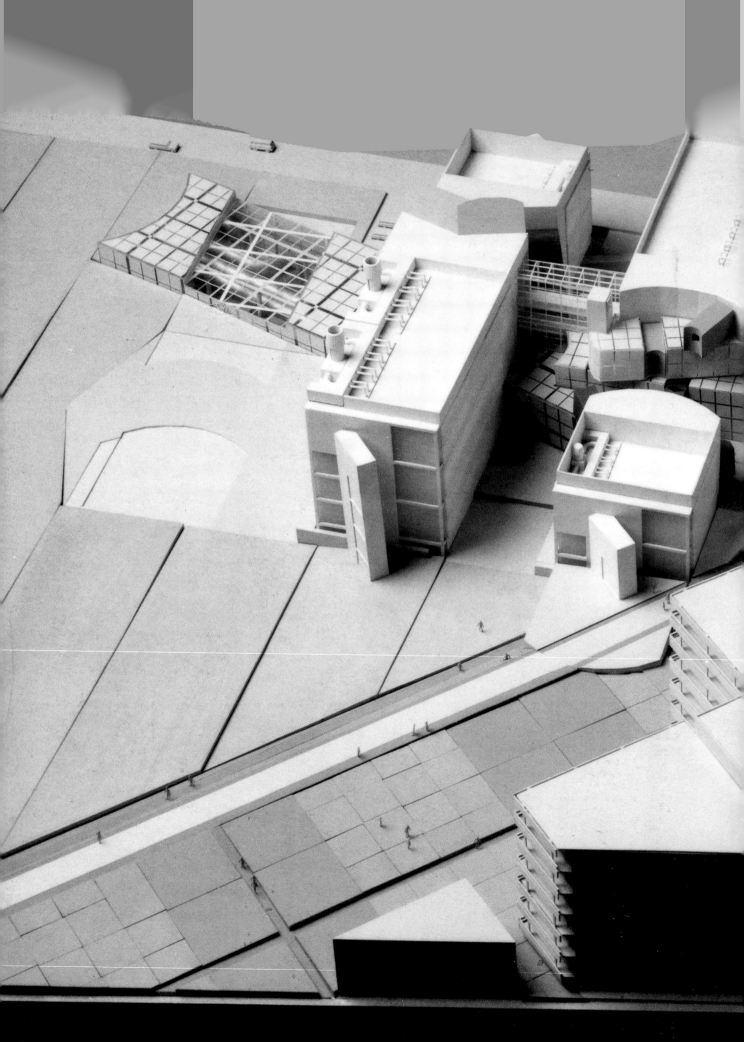

55. Site model A

56. *Basement*
57. *Roof*
58. *Second floor*
59. *Ground floor*
60. *Second subbasement*

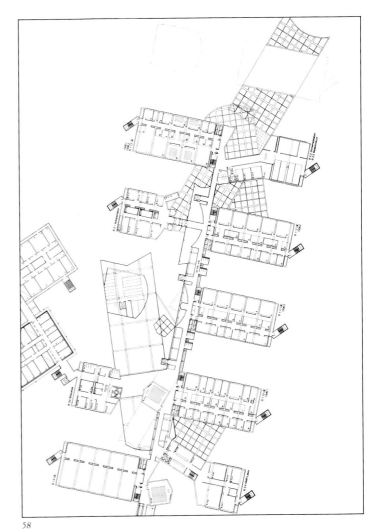

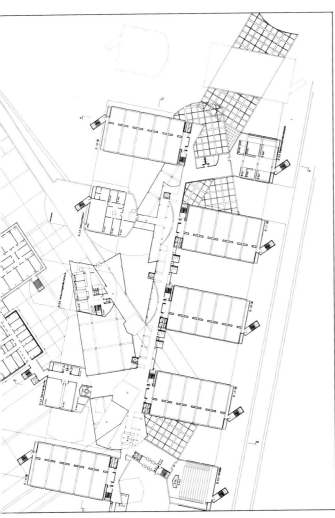

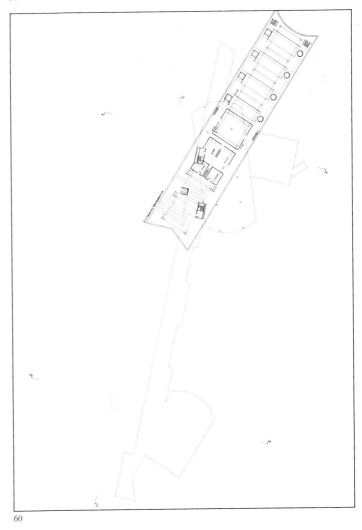

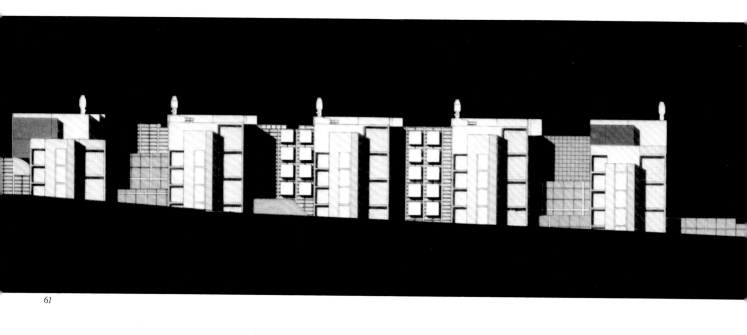

61

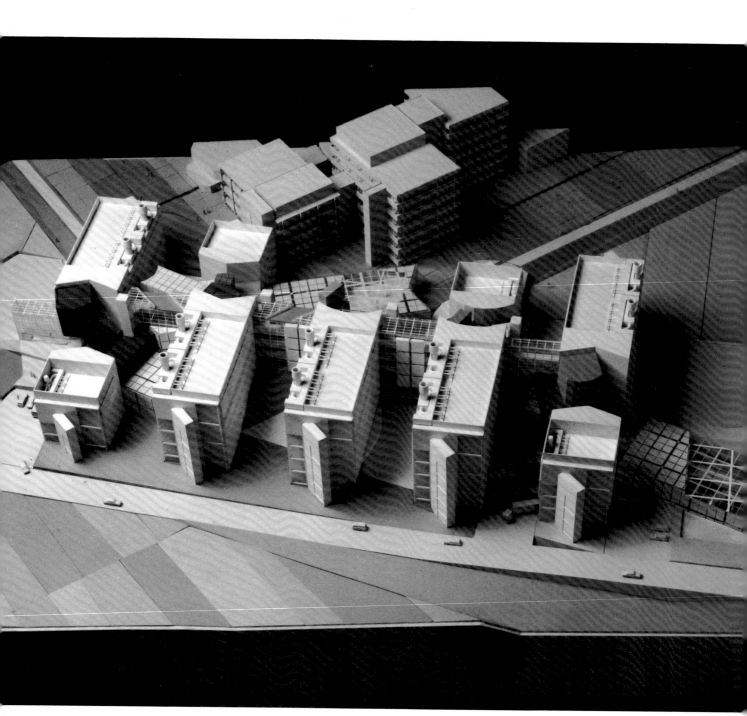

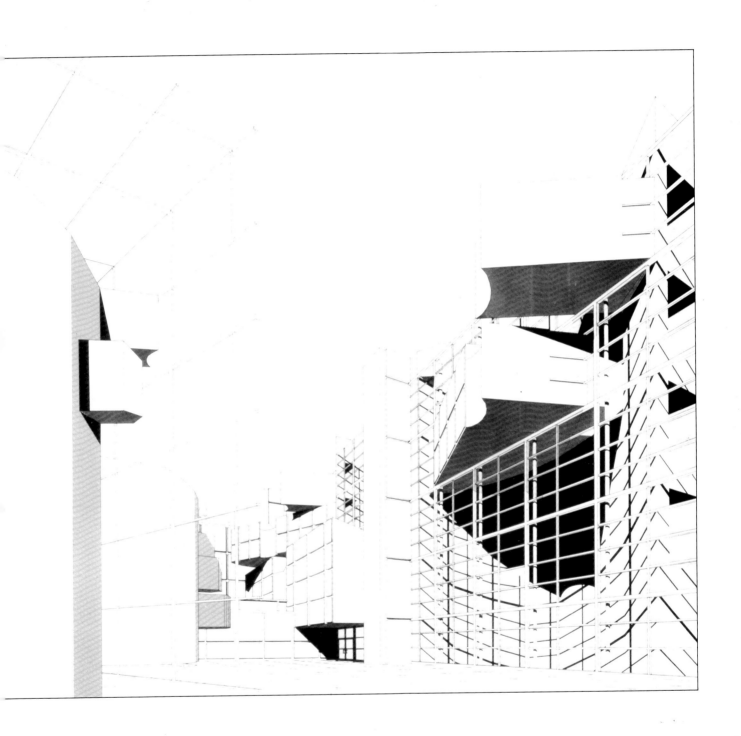

. Elevation
. Site model A
. Perspective of spine

Zaha M. Hadid

Born in Baghdad, Iraq, 1950
Based in London, England

The Peak. Hong Kong. 1982
Awarded First Prize, Hong Kong Peak Interna-
    tional Competition. 1983
Senior Designer: Michael Wolfson
Design Team: Jonathan Dunn, Marianne Van der
    Waals, Nabil Ayoubi, Alistair Standing,
    Nancy Lee, Wendy Galway
Structural Engineer: David Thomlinson
    (Ove Arup and Partners)

The Peak was the first-prize winner in a competition for a club for the wealthy in the hills above
Hong Kong harbor. The natural topography of
these hills is transformed by excavating the site to
its lowest level and constructing a set of artificial
cliffs out of the excavated rock, which is polished
to blur further the distinction between man-made
and artificial. The site is reconfigured into a
sequence of immense, abstract, polished granite
geometric forms.

Into this artificial topography are thrust four
huge beams. The beams have been abstracted from
the skyscrapers in the city below, turned over on to
their sides, brought up the hill (pl. 78), and driven
into the hillside (pl. 79) to form a horizontal sky-
scraper (pl. 80). The project's force comes from the
violent intersection between these linear beams and
the volumes of the artificial topography.

The four beams are twisted relative to each
other, bringing them into conflict with each other
as well as with the artificial landscape (pl. 64).
These conflicts disturb the internal structure of
the beams. The internal plan of each beam carries
the trace of its conflict with the other elements
(pls. 65–74). Their original subdivision into regular orthogonal units is disturbed. Closed spaces
are opened as walls are folded and buckled. The
internal grid breaks down, without ever being
abandoned. Each conflict is different, so each is
fractured in a different way, generating different
kinds of programmatic space, different types of
residential accommodation (pl. 77).

But the most radical decentering occurs when
the upper pair of beams is pulled apart, vertically,
enough from the lower pair to construct a deep
void which is completely isolated from traditional
assumptions about building. The usual hierarchies
and orthogonal order are missing. Within this
newly defined territory, building elements float,
pinned only by twisted cocktail sticks (pl. 81). In
the void are suspended entrance decks, a swimming
pool, floating platforms, snack bar, and library.
These objects break free of the regular geometry of
the beams (pl. 70).

The gap between the horizontal beams forms an
indeterminate space in which everything is angular
and joined by long diagonal ramps. A curved car
ramp sweeps up through the void (pls. 69, 82) and
into the carpark within the topmost volume.

The basic elements of the club occupy both the
void and the underground world of the artificial
topography extending back into the hillside. The
club is stretched between the emptiness of the void
and the density of the underground solids, domains
normally excluded from modern architecture but
found within it by pushing modernism to its limits, forcing it apart. In this way, the pleasure palace, the hedonist resort, is located in the twisted
center of modernist purity.

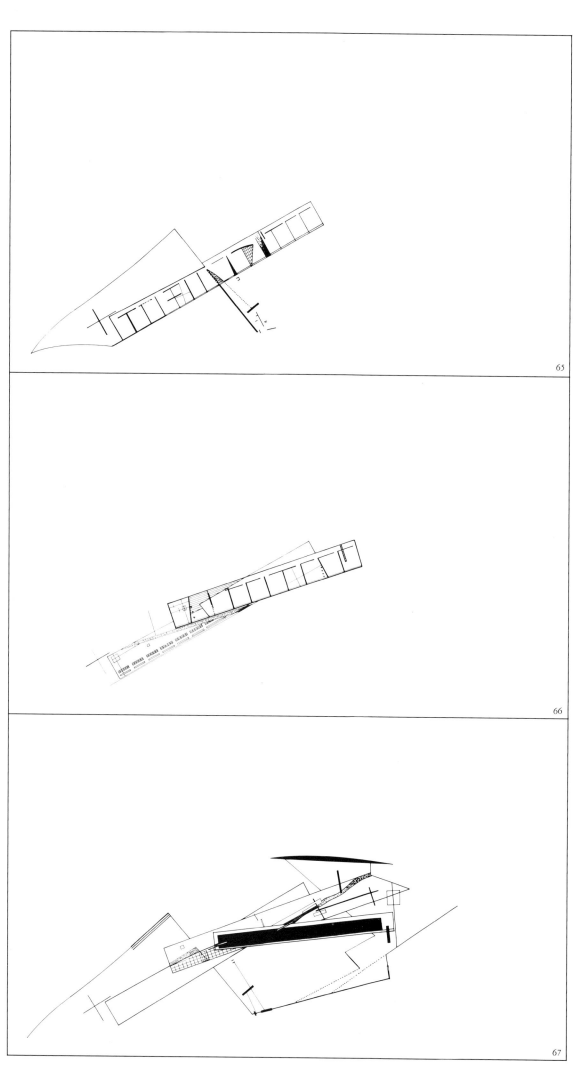

The Peak
64. (Overleaf) Site plan
65. First (lowest) beam
66. Second beam, resting on
first beam
67. Club deck, roof of second
beam
68. Lower layer of void
69. Upper layer of void,
showing car ramp
70. Elements suspended
in void

65

66

67

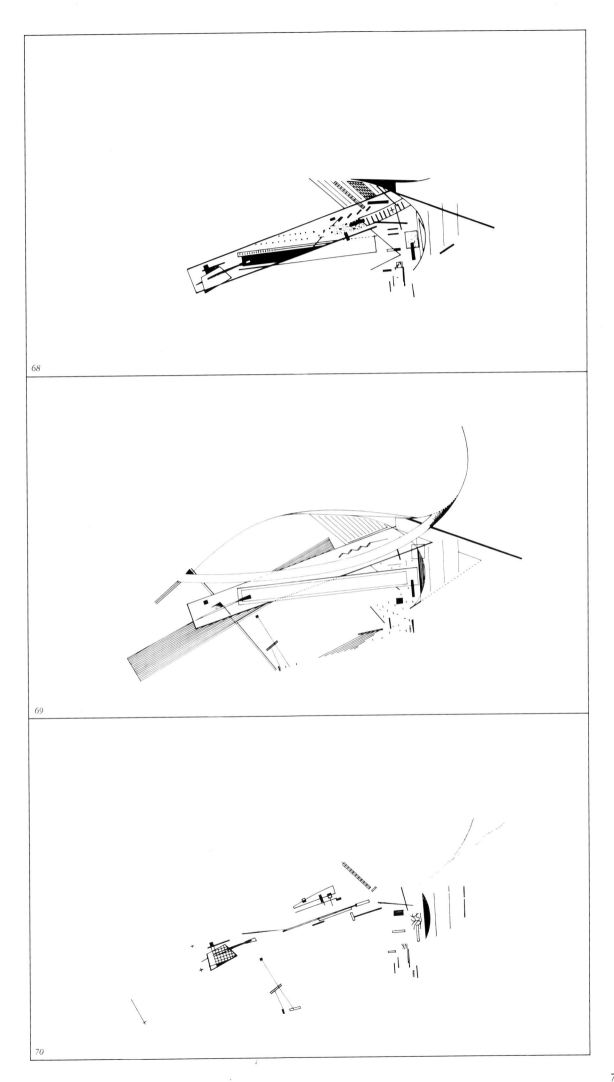

68

69

70

71

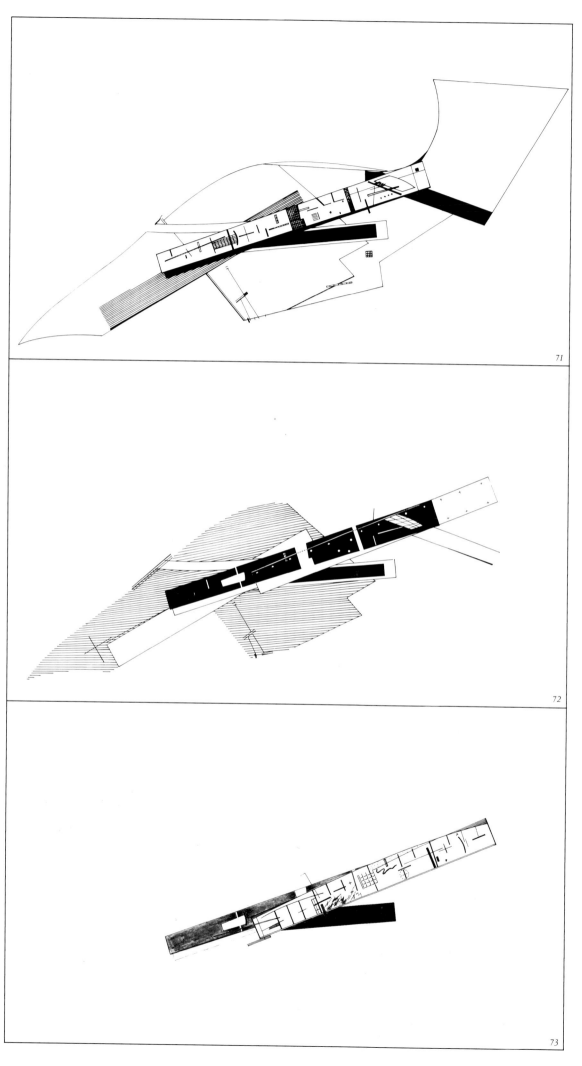

71. Third beam, above
72. Deck between third
fourth beams
73. Fourth beam
74. Deck on roof of four
beam
75. Composite of beams
76. Composite of suspen
elements within and bet
beams

71

72

73

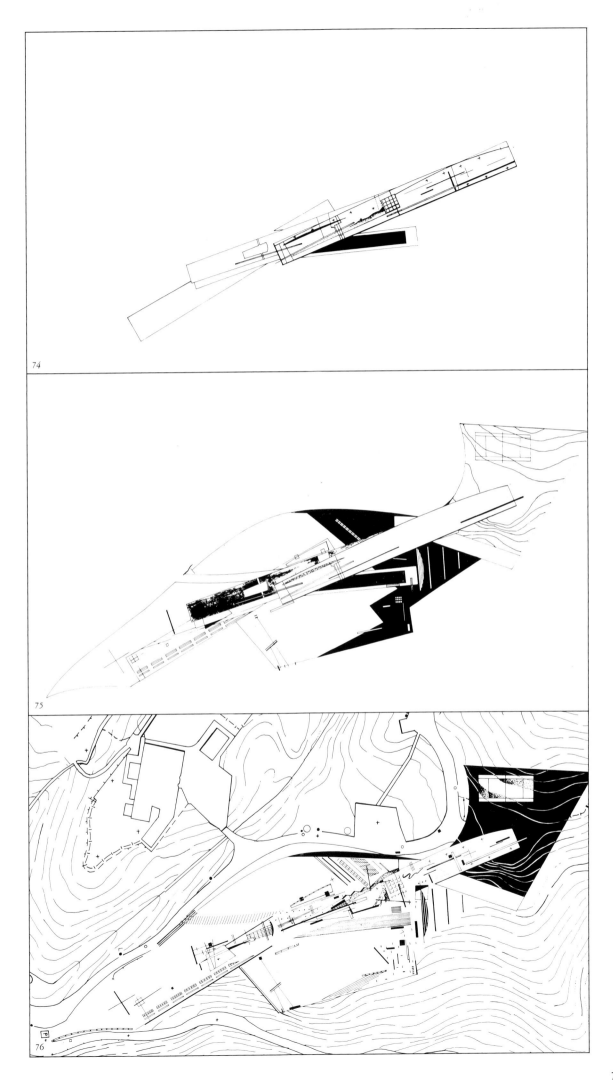

74

75

76

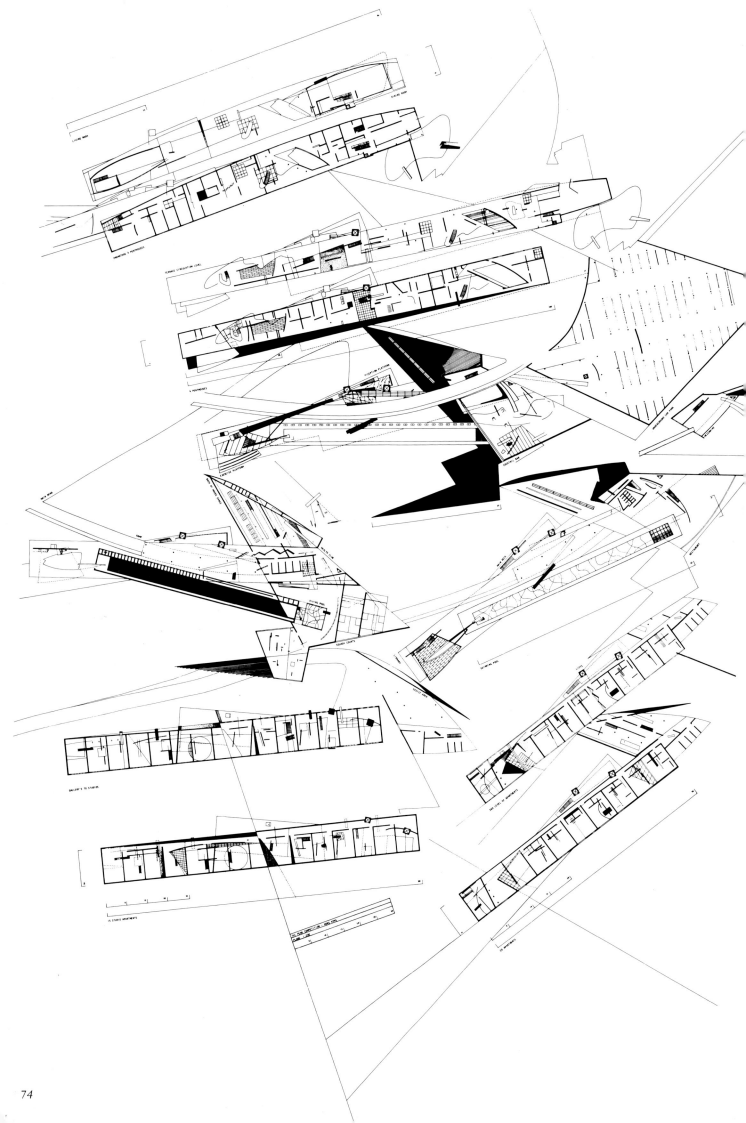

74

78

79

*80. Rendering of project
in context*

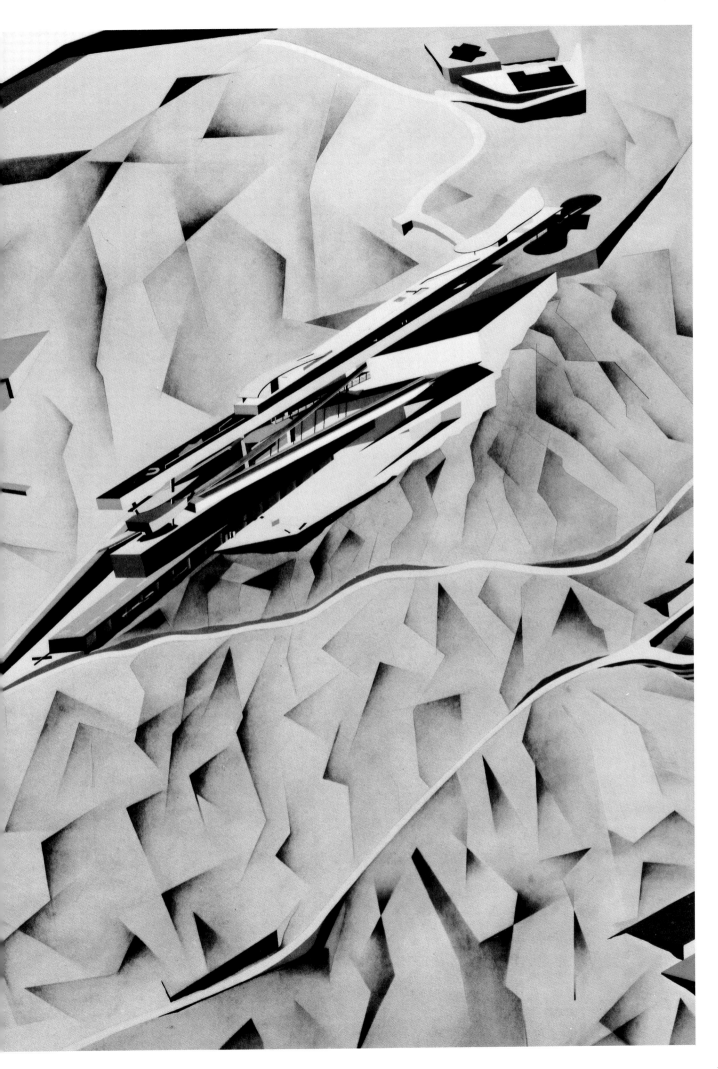

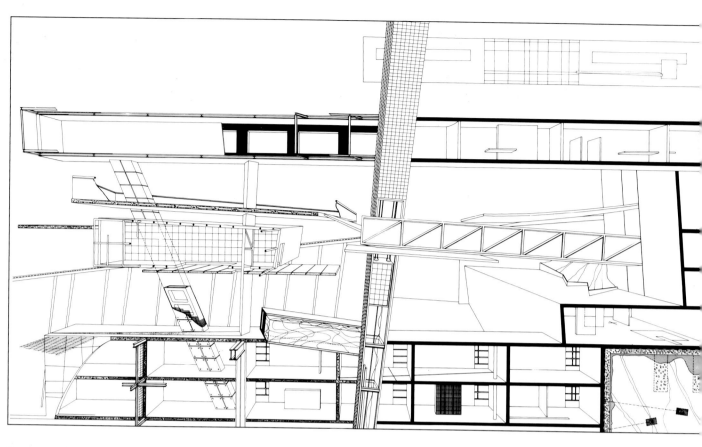

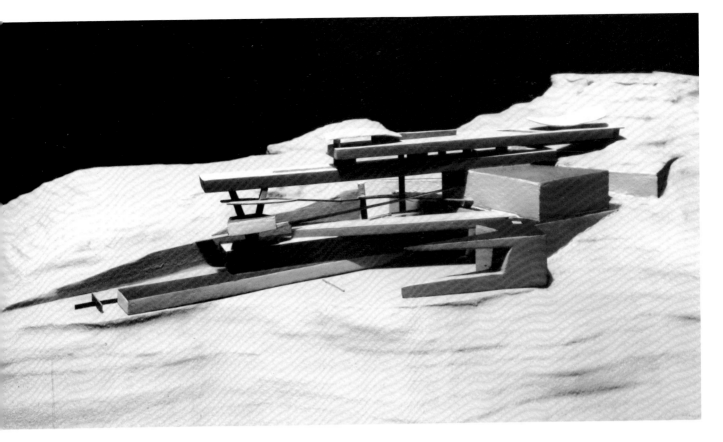

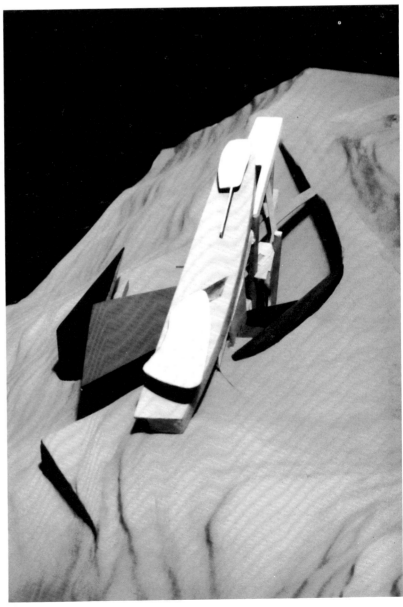

81. *Section through elements suspended in void*
82. *Perspective of elements suspended in void*
83, 84. *Site model*

84

Coop Himmelblau
Based in Vienna, Austria

Wolf D. Prix
Born in Vienna, Austria, 1942

Helmut Swiczinsky
Born in Poznań, Poland, 1944

Rooftop Remodeling. Vienna, Austria. 1985
Design Team: Franz Sam, Stefan Krüger, Karin
 Sam, Katharina Lenz, Max Pauly
Structural Engineer: Oskar Graf

Apartment Building. Vienna, Austria. 1986
Design Team: Frank Stepper, Fritz Mascher,
 Franz Sam

Skyline. Hamburg, Federal Republic of
 Germany. 1985
Design Team: Friedrike Brauneck, Michael van
 Ooyen, Franz Sam, Frank Stepper, Fritz
 Mascher
Structural Engineer: Oskar Graf

The rooftop remodeling (pls. 85–89) is a renovation of 4,300 square feet of attic space of a traditional apartment block in Vienna. The stable form has been infected by an unstable biomorphic structure, a skeletal winged organism which distorts the form that houses it. Yet the new structure is also tense and taut, highly sprung, a metallic construction whose apparently chaotic form results from a close analysis of the larger structure it inhabits. Consequently, it is not only a wing—a means of flight, a source of lift—but also a leading edge—a cutting edge, a blade—which slices through the corner and springs outside. The stable relationship between inside and outside is jeopardized.

The other Vienna project (pls. 90–99) is a fifty-unit apartment building on a main street leading out of the city. It sets in conflict four suspended bars, which are twisted in all dimensions. The internal structure of each bar is disturbed by the conflict with the other bars, and each is distorted. The intersection of the pure bars produces warped spaces, an internal impurity: a contorted interior organized by a system of lifts, stairways, and a ramp which ascends diagonally through the complex. The building leans over precariously, in tension with the basic rhythm of horizontal floor planes. It is held together by vertical shafts, and stabilized by angled struts. The skin of the bars is cut open and peeled back to expose this twisted structure.

The skyline tower (pls. 100–106) is part of a refurbishment plan for the banks of the Elbe in Hamburg. It is one of a complex of five buildings that straddle the river, a thousand-foot-tall tower propped up by huge columns. Suspended above the ground, it frustrates traditional expectations about towers: it is thinner at the base than the top; and rather than being a monolith, it is splintering—radical fissures open up, cleaving the building into pieces that slide up and down along lines of shear. They break into sharp points which buckle, split, and peel back to expose the regular layers of floor planes. This produces a confusion of overlapping eccentric spaces within which the functions are organized. The structure is held together by stressed ligaments which bind each element to the system of columns: the building is firmly held on the edge of apparent collapse.

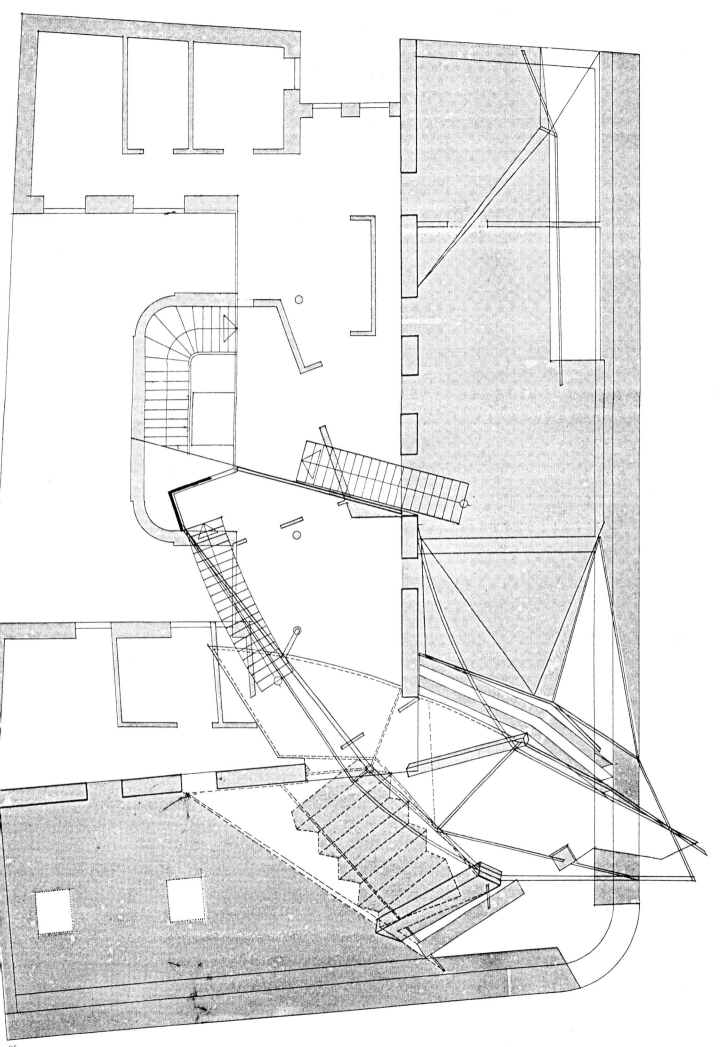

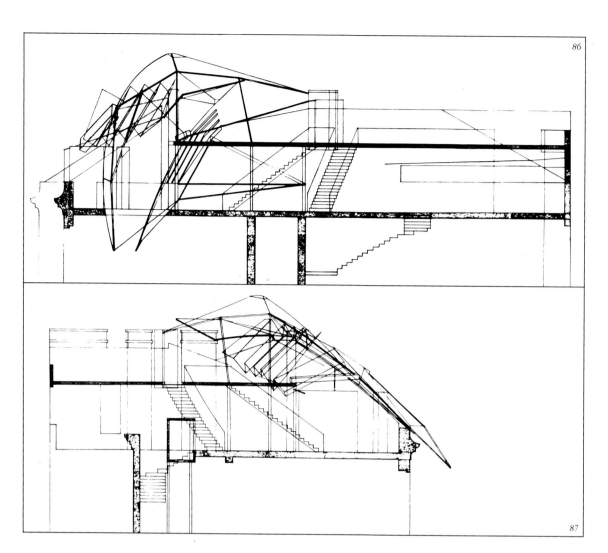

Rooftop Remodeling
85. *(Overleaf) Roof plan*
86. *Longitudinal section*
87. *Transverse section*
88. *Structural model*
89. *Site model*

87

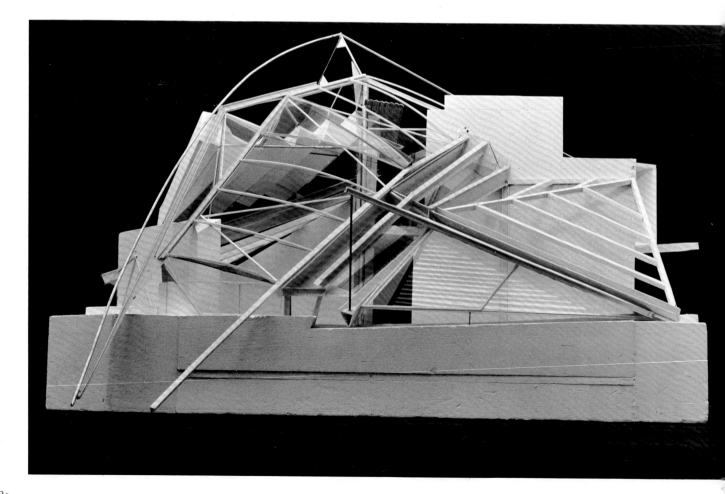

Apartment Building
0. Study model
1. Structural model
2. Final model
3. Detail of final model

93

85

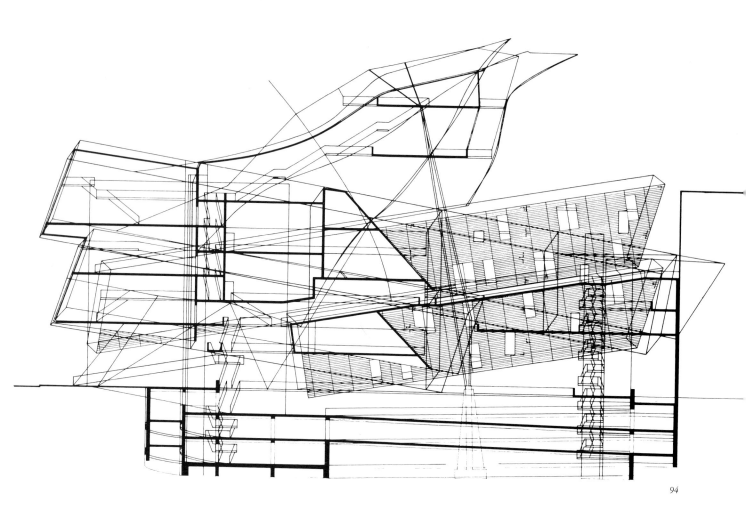

94

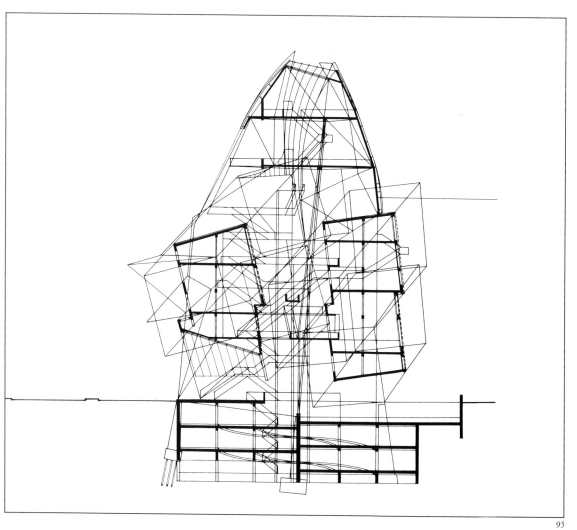

94. *Longitudinal section*
95. *Transverse section*
96–99. *Floor plans,*
highest to lowest level

95

96

97

98

99

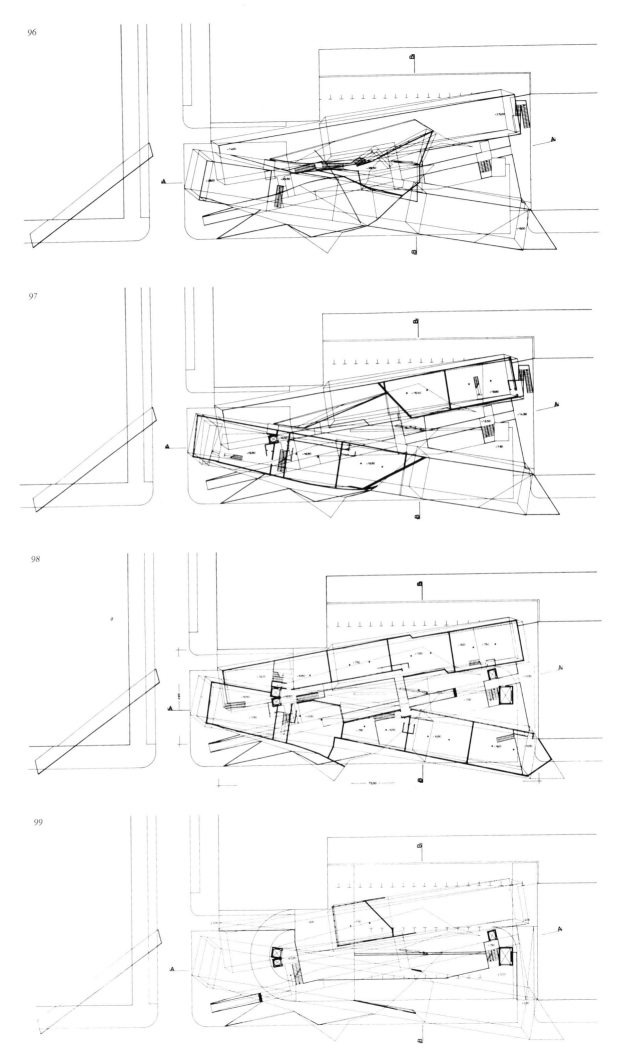

103

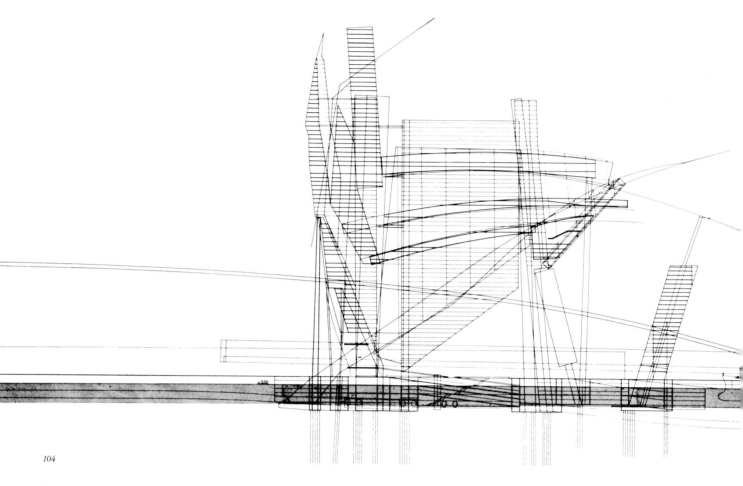

104

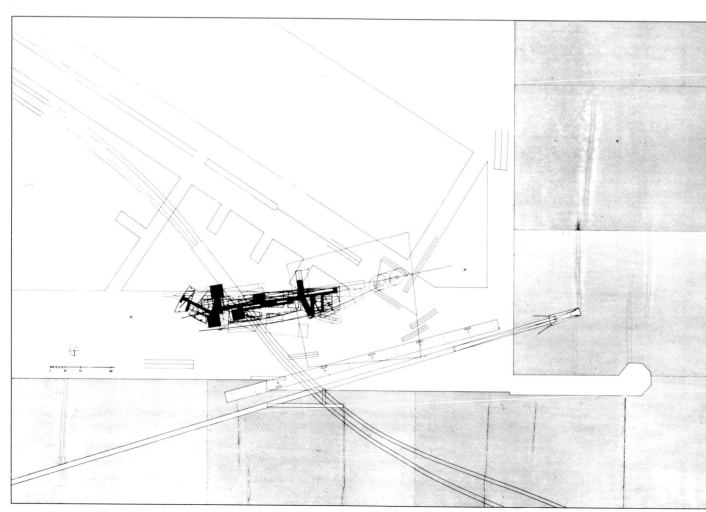

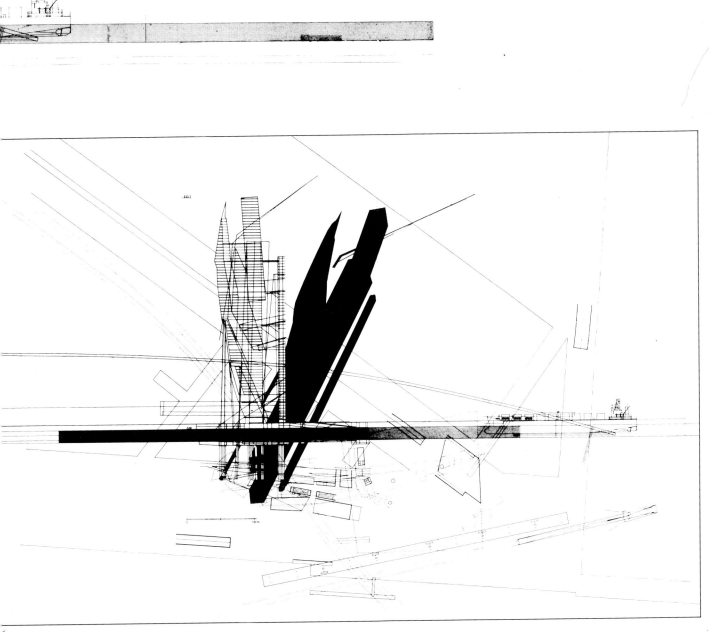

Bernard Tschumi

Born in Lausanne, Switzerland, 1944
Based in New York, New York

Parc de La Villette. Paris, France. 1982–85
Awarded First Prize, Parc de La Villette
    International Competition. 1983
Competition Design. 1982–83
    Associate: Luca Merlini
Developed Design. 1983–84
    Associate: Colin Fournier
    Design Team: Luca Merlini, Alexandra
    Villegas, Neil Porter, Steve MacAdam
Final Design. 1985
    Associate: Jean-François Erhel
    Design Team: Alexandra Villegas,
    Ursula Kurz
    Structural Engineer: Peter Rice (Ove Arup
    and Partners), with Hugh Dutton

This project is a public park occupying the 125 acres of La Villette in Paris. The park is populated by an array of scattered structures linked by a complex series of gardens, axial galleries, and meandering promenades.

The basic principle of the project is the superimposition of three autonomous ordering systems: points, lines, and surfaces (pl. 107). The system of points is established by a grid of ten-meter cubes. The system of lines is a set of classical axes. The system of surfaces is a set of pure geometric figures: circle, square, and triangle. Independently, each system begins as an idealized structure, a traditional mechanism of order. But when superimposed they sometimes produce distortion (through interference), sometimes reinforcement, and sometimes indifference. The result is a series of ambiguous intersections between systems, a domain of complex events—a domain of play—in which the status both of ideal forms and traditional composition is challenged. Ideals of purity, perfection, and order become sources of impurity, imperfection, and disorder.

Each system is distorted by the conflict with other systems but is also distorted within itself. The galleries defined by axes are twisted and broken (pls. 112, 113). The pure figures of the surfaces are warped. Each of the cubes is decomposed into a number of formal elements which are then variously recombined (pls. 114, 115). The result is that each point of the grid is marked by a different permutation of the same object (pl. 116).

In each structure (pls. 118–132), the cube remains legible. But the dismembered cube is not simply reassembled into a number of new stable forms, by rearranging the kit of parts. Instead, the elements are embedded in each other in unstable assemblages: they are placed in conflict with each other and with the cube. The cube has been distorted by elements that were extracted from it. These distorted cubes are then deformed further (pl. 117) in order to accommodate different functions (restaurant, arcade, and so on). They become follies in the park: freestanding structures linked by broken galleries that twist through a fractured topography.

The park is an elaborate essay in the deviation of ideal forms. It gains its force by turning each distortion of an ideal form into a new ideal, which is then itself distorted. With each new generation of distortion, the trace of the previous ideal remains, producing a convoluted archeology, a history of successive idealizations and distortions. In this way, the park destabilizes pure architectural form.

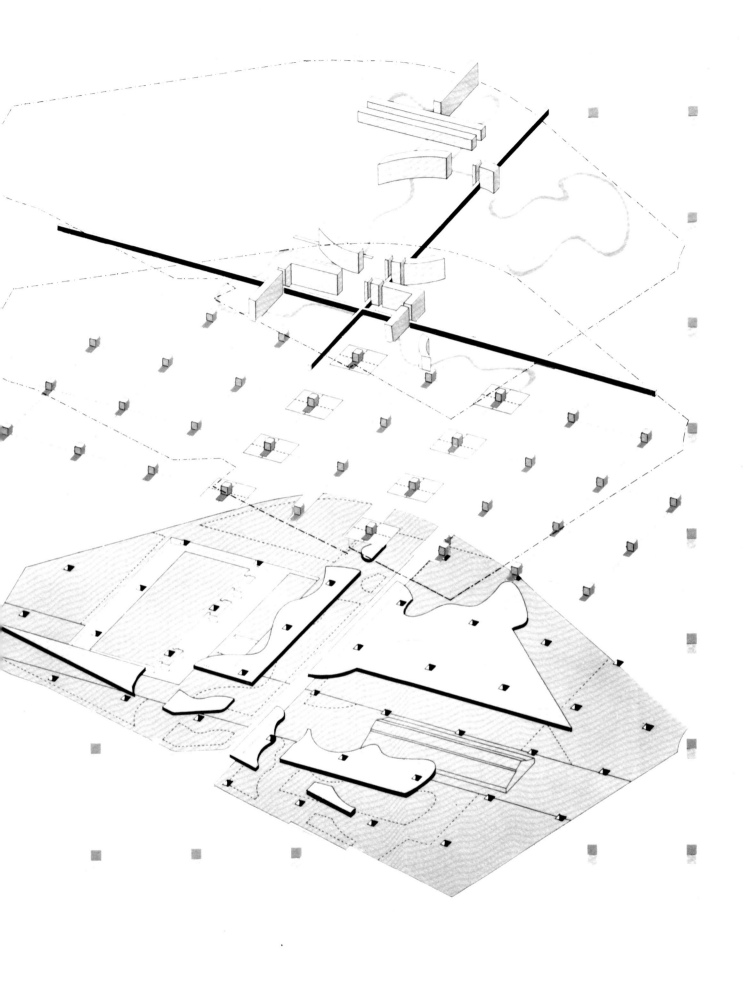

93

*107. (Overleaf) Axono-
metric; superimposition of
points, lines, and surfaces*

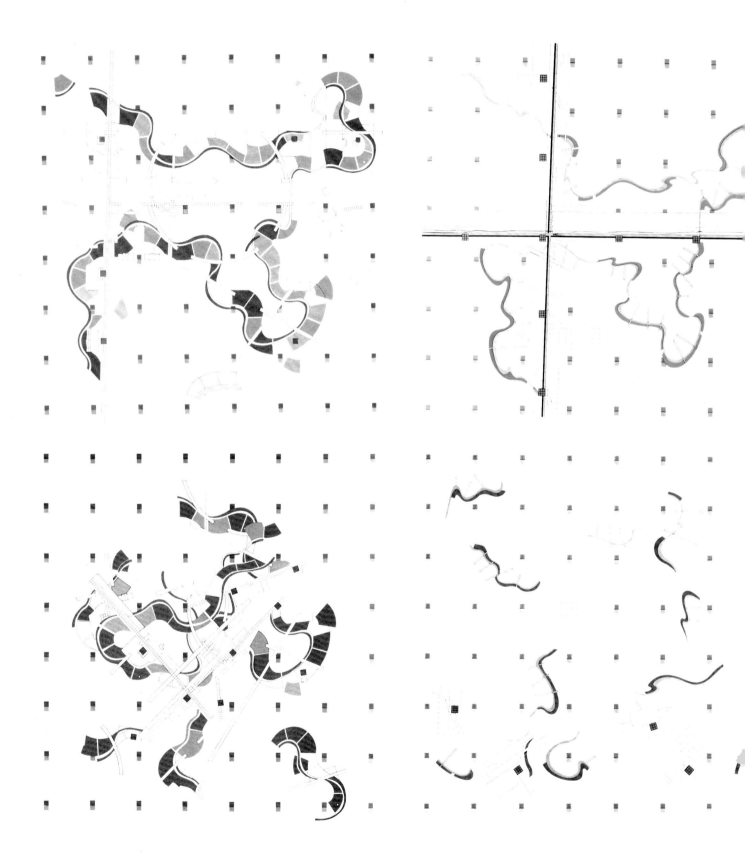

108. Sequence of gardens
109. Deviation

110. Promenade
111. Deviation

94

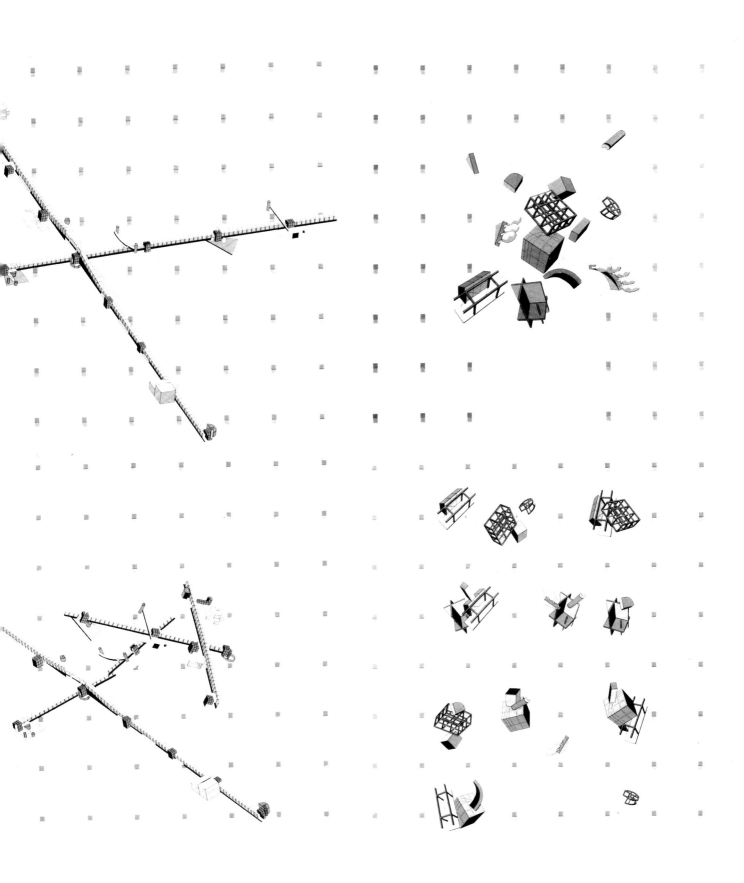

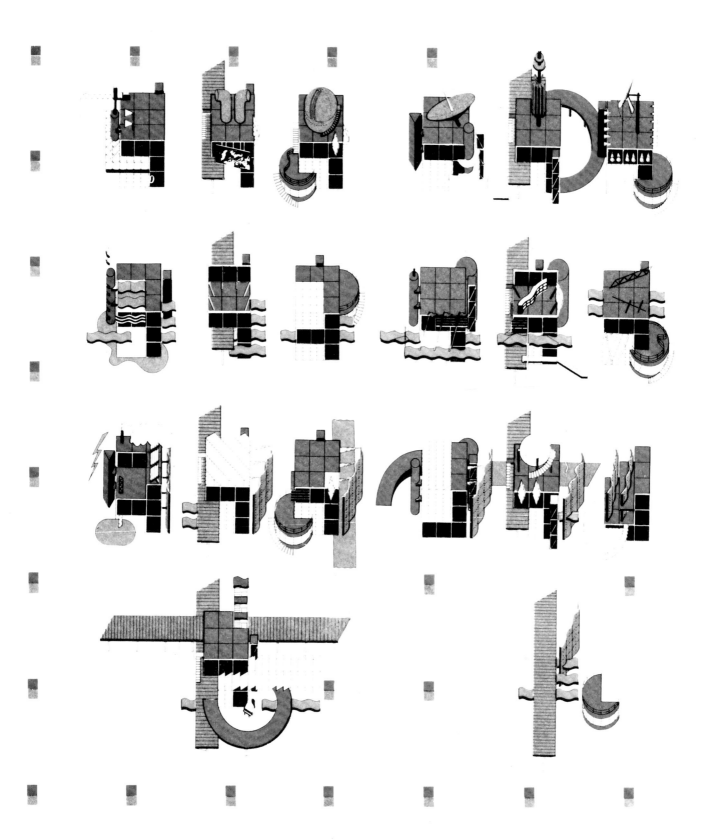

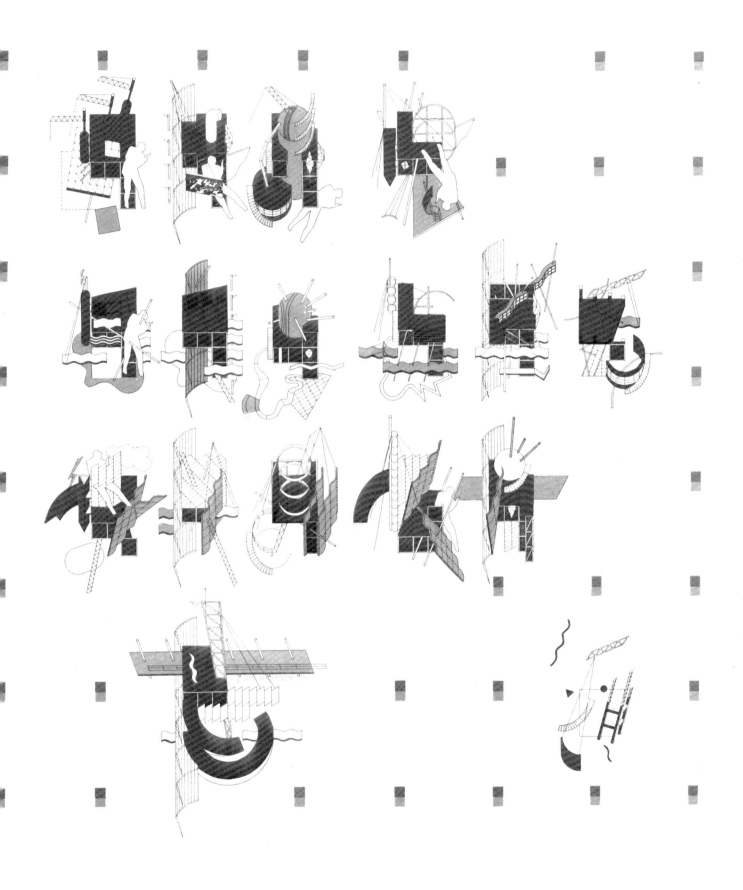

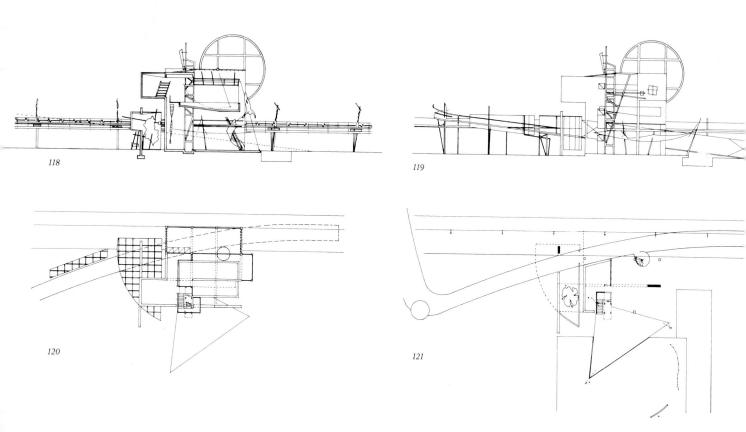

118

119

120

121

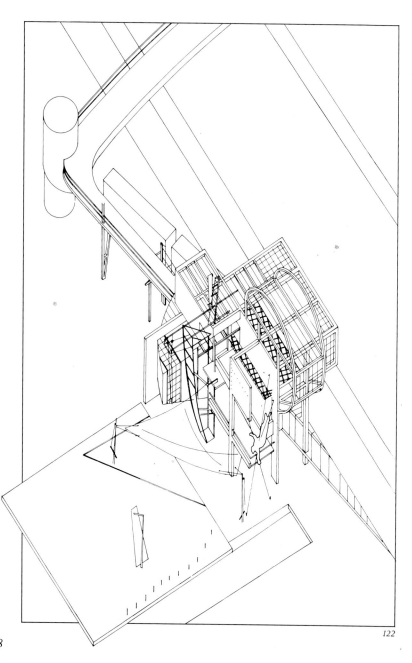

122

Folly N5, deviation
118. *Section*
119. *Elevation*
120. *Mezzanine*
121. *Ground floor*
122. *Axonometric*

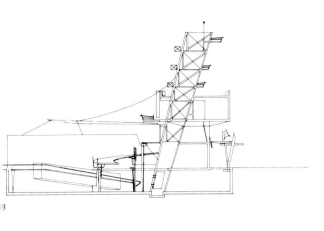

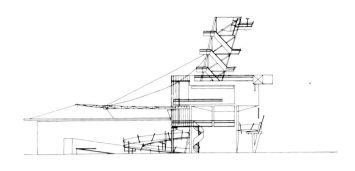

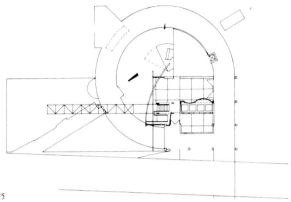

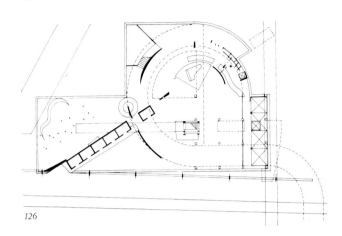

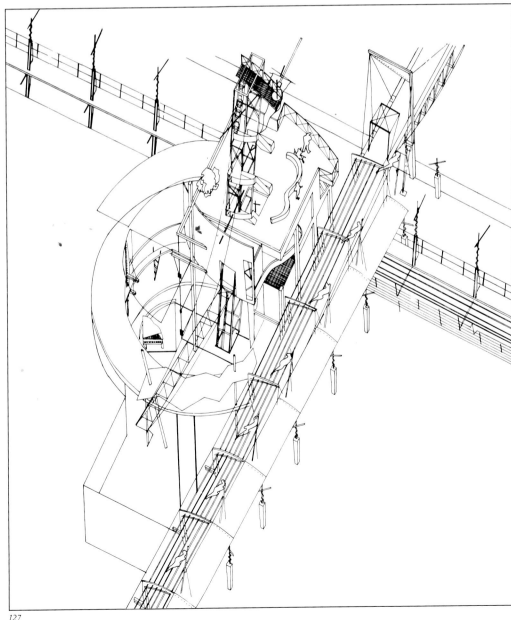

Folly L5, deviation
23. *Section*
24. *Elevation*
25. *Second floor*
26. *Basement*
27. *Axonometric*

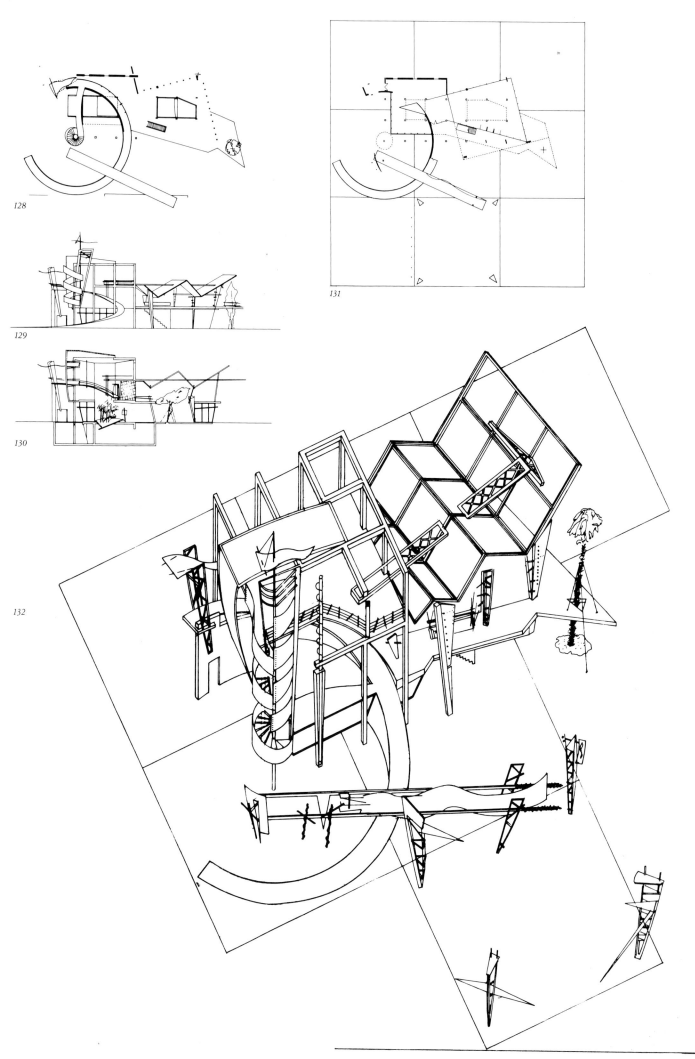

128

129

130

131

132

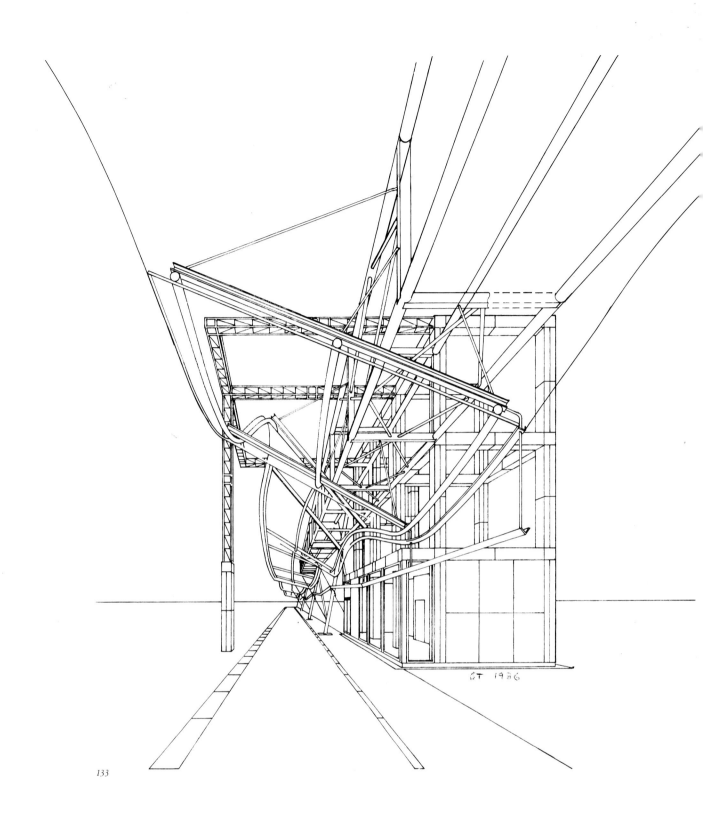

133

Photograph Credits

Photographs reproduced in this book were provided, in the majority of cases, by the architects and their offices, as cited in the project listings and captions. The following list applies to photographs for which a separate acknowledgment is due.

© Hélène Binet: pls. 27, 32, 34
Tom Bonner: pls. 1, 3, 5, 7, 8, 10, 11, 12
Dennis Cowley, courtesy Max Protetch Gallery, New York: pl. 36
© 1987, 1988 Dick Frank Studio, Inc.: pls. 46, 48, 49, 55, 62
Robert Hahn, Vienna: pl. 88
© Hectic Pictures/Hans Werlemann: pls. 37, 38, 45
Michael Heizer: p. 8, bottom
Frank Hellwig, courtesy ANF, Kassel: pl. 50
Gordon Matta-Clark, courtesy Galerie Lelong, New York: fig. 3
© The Museum of Modern Art, New York, photograph by Seth Joel: p. 8, top
Susan Narduli and Perry Blake: pl. 9
Brian D. Nicholson: pls. 22, 25
© Uwe Rau, Berlin: pls. 26, 30, 31, 33
© 1977 SITE Projects, Inc.: fig. 2
Tim Street-Porter: pls. 14, 15, 16, 17
Clay Tudor: pl. 18
Edward Woodman: pls. 83, 84
© Gerald Zugmann, Vienna: pls. 89, 90, 91, 92, 93, 102, 103